STAR TREK®
Paper Universe

ANDREW PANG

POCKET BOOKS

New York   London   Sydney   Singapore

An *Original* Publication of POCKET BOOKS

 POCKET BOOKS, a division of Simon & Schuster, Inc.
1230 Avenue of the Americas, New York, NY 10020

This book is published by Pocket Books, a division of Simon & Schuster, Inc., under exclusive license from Paramount Pictures.

ISBN: 0-671-04215-7

First Pocket Books trade paperback printing September 2000

10 9 8 7 6 5 4 3 2 1

POCKET and colophon are registered tradmarks of Simon & Schuster, Inc.

Designed by Kris Tobiassen

Printed in the U.S.A

For my parents,
John & Helen
and always,
Sarah

In memory of my
dearest friend,
Shelly Bayman Lageyne

U.S.S. Enterprise NCC-1701

U.S.S. Enterprise NCC-1701-A

U.S.S. Enterprise NCC-1701-D

U.S.S. Enterprise NCC-1701-E

U.S.S. Defiant NX-74205

U.S.S. Voyager NCC-74656

Shuttlecraft Type-6

Shuttlecraft Type-9

Deep Space 9

Klingon Battle Cruiser

Klingon Bird-of-Prey

Borg Cube

Ferengi Marauder

Cardassian *Galor*-class
Warship

Jem'Hadar Attack Ship

Romulan Bird-of-Prey

Contents

ALLIED VESSELS AND STATION

SHIPS OF THE GALAXY

Introduction

Origami is a Japanese word, made up of two characters, *ori* (folding) and *gami* (paper). This modern day pastime dates back to sixth-century Japan, though the Eastern Han Dynasty of China first developed paper itself in about 105 A.D. As paper was costly to make, the art of folding was mostly used for symbolic and ceremonial purposes. The idea behind this book is to merge one of the oldest and most popular pastimes together with the wonderful science fiction world of *Star Trek* created by Gene Roddenberry back in the sixties.

The biggest challenge in origami is to achieve the ideal results by adhering to the rules, but rules are made to be broken. In fact, contrary to modern day origami, whereby the strictest rule allows only the folding of a single square, the traditional folders frequently used cuts and glue in their models. Depending on the final result and the purpose—cutting, gluing and a variation of shapes in paper also have their place in origami. As origami becomes a more international pastime, I strongly believe it should first and foremost be fun; it should be able to appeal to a larger audience, and to demonstrate that paper is one of the most versatile materials.

This book features sixteen popular starships from the *Star Trek* universe, covering ships from the original television series to the latest movies. In this book, you will find models that are made up of more than one piece of paper, and models that are folded from triangular-shaped paper. Although these methods are slightly unconventional, I believe you will be happy with the results.

Finally, it is up to you to discover the wonderful world of origami by studying the signs, symbols, bases, and most importantly, practice, practice, practice. I hope you will have as much fun in folding these models as I have had in creating them.

Symbols

The symbols used in this book are based on the international symbols developed by Akira Yoshizawa. Once you have memorized these symbols, you will have no problem in following the instructions and diagrams. In addition to the symbols in the diagrams, I have also provided written instructions on each step to assist you in understanding the illustrations.

Remember that origami is an art form based on geometry. So follow the symbols and instructions carefully as there is little tolerance for error in the folding process.

Basic Folds

There are several standard folds that have developed in origami over the years; these folds are used in conjunction with some of the symbols. For example, you will encounter the sink fold, the inside reverse fold, and the crimp fold among others. When you are instructed to use folds that you do not understand, go back to the Basic Folds and Bases chapter and look for the examples.

In this book, apart from the simple hill and valley folds, the most commonly used basic folds are the sink, inside, and outside reverse folds. So, study them well before attempting to fold the models.

Bases

In this section, you will find traditional bases (the bird base, the preliminary base, and the water bomb base) and bases created by me (starbase 1 and 2). Many famous origami models are created starting with these bases.

Also, the instructions use these bases as a kind of shortcut or reference in the illustrations. You may need to refer back to this section before and during each folding of the models. For example, the original *Starship Enterprise*, *Enterprise-A* and the Romulan bird-of-prey all begin with one of the bases I have created. So, practice and get familiar with these bases.

Paper

Almost any paper can be used to fold an origami model. Traditional origami paper is colored on one side and white on the other. Remember—better paper makes a better model.

Today commercial origami paper is available in a variety of different colors, patterns, and sizes. This paper comes in sizes from as small as 75mm by 75mm to the more popular sizes of 150mm by 150mm and 170mm by 170mm. I prefer to use paper that has the same color on both sides. All the models in this book are based on using this type of paper. This paper tends to be a lot larger and usually comes in a rectangular shape, which allows you to cut out as big or small a piece as you desire.

For this book, I would suggest you use a larger piece of paper for practice as some parts of the models could get very tight for smaller paper. In fact, gift-wrapping paper, photocopy paper, typing, or computer paper are all excellent types for practice. So, experiment with them and try them out for yourself.

Once you have mastered the models, you could try gluing kitchen aluminum foil in between two pieces of thin paper. The result would be models that are very solid and easy to bend in the shape you desire. For this exercise, I used some commercially available paper, which has a slightly rough-textured surface, giving an 'alien' feel to the models. Choose thinner paper or the models may become too bulky.

This type of paper gives an "alien" feel to the models.

Equipment

RETRACTABLE BLADE—Often called the cutter. Use this to trim or slice paper into shape. Use ones with the plastic handle as they are safer to hold.

CUTTING MAT—Place paper on top of the cutting mat before slicing, thus preventing damage to tabletops beneath.

GLUE—Although it is not encouraged for use, glue sometimes can enhance the look of the finished models, as it keeps everything in place.

TWEEZERS—Very helpful to fold tight places for the more complex models.

Now, boldly fold where no one has folded before!

—Andrew Pang
Hong Kong
March 2000

Symbols

— — — — — **valley fold**

—·· — ·· — ·· — **hill fold**

enlarged diagram

sink fold

push

precrease paper

repeat a step one or more times

cut

turn over

zigzag

crimp

inflate

·············· **X-ray lines**

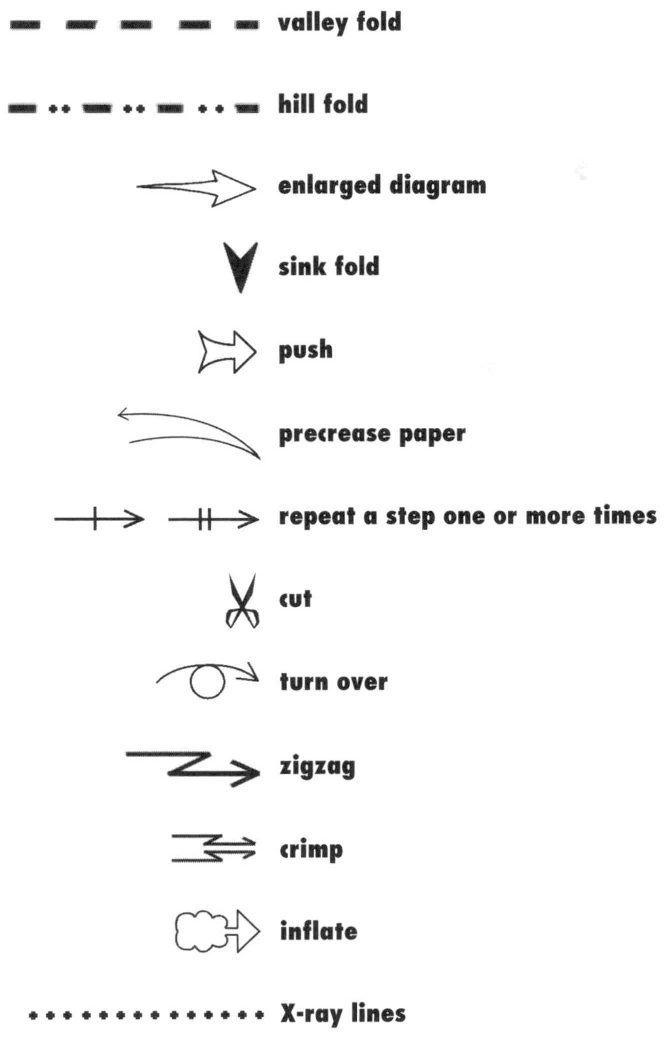

Basic Folds and Bases

**Practicing and understanding these folds is important
and you can practice these folds on any size paper.**

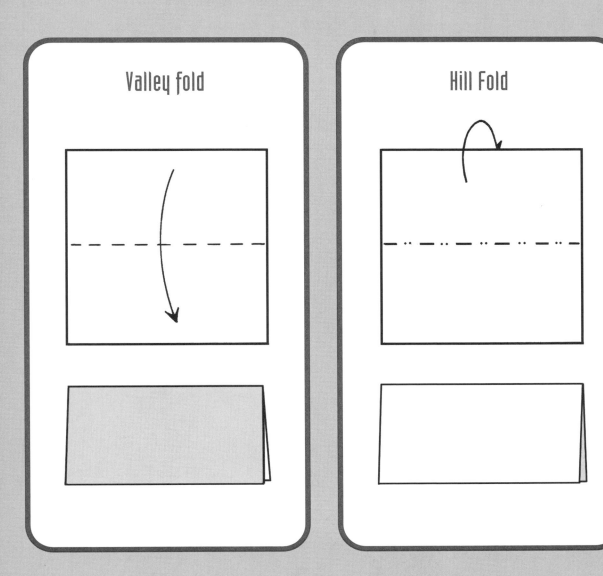

Zigzag/Step Fold

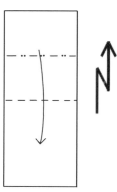

1 Valley fold paper downward.

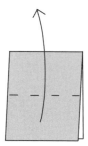

2 Valley fold paper upward.

3 A completed zigzag/step fold.

TIP: You don't need to practice this fold on rectangular paper.

Inside Reverse fold

1 This is a hill fold.

2 Continue to push upward.

3 Completed inside reverse.

TIP: The shaded side represents the front side of the paper.

Outside Reverse fold

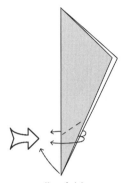

1 This is a valley fold.

2 Continue to flip upward.

3 Completed outside reverse.

Squash Fold

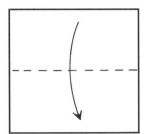

1 Valley fold paper in half.

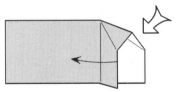

2 Precrease paper—first hill fold corner section backward and hill fold across.

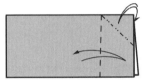

3 Fold across the top layer of the precreased valley fold and squash open the precreased corner section.

4 Fold flat to complete the squash.

Crimp Fold

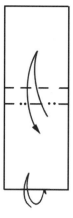

1 Precrease valley fold and then hill fold.

2 Fold paper across in half.

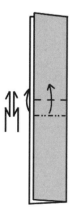

3 It is in fact a double zigzag fold.

4 A completed 'crimp' fold.

TIP: You don't need to practice this fold on rectangular paper.

Rabbit's Ear Fold

1 Valley fold across at the diagonal line to precrease paper.

2 Precrease with valley folding lower left-hand edge to meet the diagonal crease.

3 Repeat the same fold on the lower right-hand edge.

4 Valley fold across the vertical diagonal line to precrease paper.

5 Lift the bottom left and right edges upward and valley fold inward.

6 This will cause the center section to form a small triangular hill.

7 Flatten the triangular hill to complete the fold.

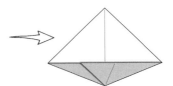

8 Completed rabbit's ear.

Water Bomb Base

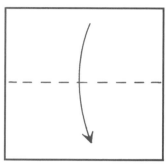

1 Begin with a square piece of paper. Valley fold paper in half.

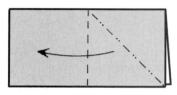

2 Pull across the upper layer from the halfway line and squash open pocket.

TIP: Precrease valley fold and hill fold before folding across.

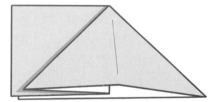

3 Turn over and repeat on the other side.

TIP: As in Step 2, precrease the paper prior to the actual fold.

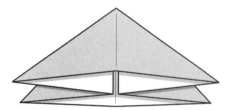

4 Squash flat to complete a water bomb base.

5 Completed water bomb base.

Preliminary Base

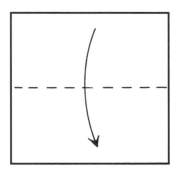

1 Begin with a square piece of paper. Valley fold paper in half.

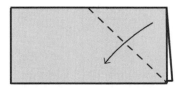

2 Valley fold right corner down to the bottom edge.

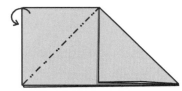

3 Hill fold the other corner down to the bottom edge on the opposite side.

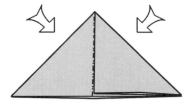

4 Open up the center pocket by pushing in from both sides.

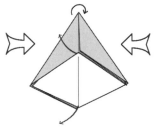

5 Intermediate step—continue to open up, rotate paper around, and squash model flat.

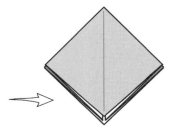

6 Completed preliminary base.

Sink Fold

Practice the fold by using a water bomb base (directions shown here as steps 1–5).

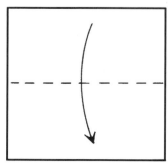

1 Begin with a square piece of paper. Valley fold paper in half.

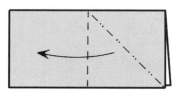

2 Pull across the upper layer from the halfway line and squash open pocket.

TIP: Precrease valley fold and hill fold before folding across.

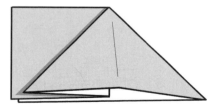

3 Turn over and repeat steps on the other side.

TIP: As in Step 2, precrease the paper prior to the actual fold.

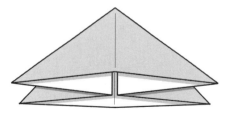

4 Squash flat to complete a water bomb base.

5 Completed water bomb base for practicing a sink fold.

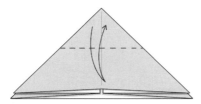

6 Precrease the top corner, then turn over the base to repeat the precrease on the other side.

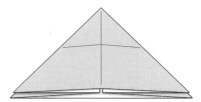

7 Reopen the paper completely.

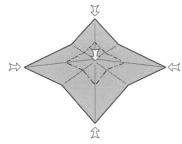

8 Push down the middle square, and at the same time close in the sides to collapse the middle square area.

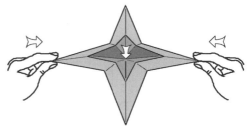

9 Slowly close paper back to collapse the middle square until it is inverted inside the model.

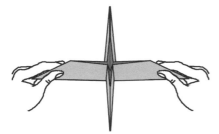

10 The middle square is now completely inverted inside the model. Fold paper flat to complete the fold.

11 Completed Sink.

Bird Base

Begin with a preliminary base (directions shown here as steps 1a–1f).

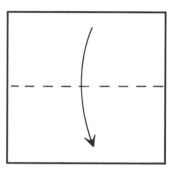

1a Begin with a square piece of paper. Valley fold paper in half.

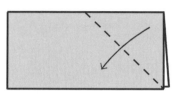

1b Valley fold right corner down to the bottom edge.

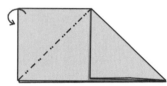

1c Hill fold the other corner down to the bottom edge on the opposite side.

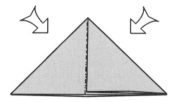

1d Open up the center pocket by pushing in from both sides.

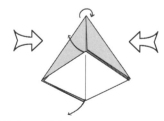

1e Intermediate step—continue to open up, rotate paper around, and squash model flat.

1f Completed preliminary base.

1 Precrease lines as indicated.

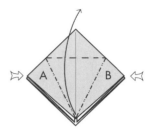

2 Lift up front flap and push in areas A and B toward center.

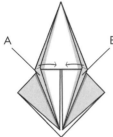

3 Intermediate step, continue to push in areas A and B toward center.

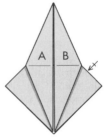

4 Turn over, repeat Steps 1 to 4 on the other side.

5 Completed bird base.

Starbase 1

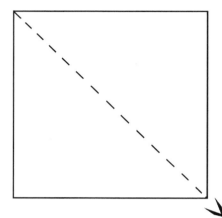

1 Begin with a square piece of paper. Make a diagonal crease and cut at dotted line to create two isosceles triangles.

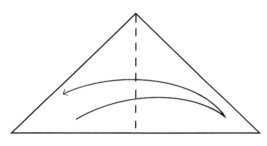

2 Take one of the triangles and precrease at the centerline.

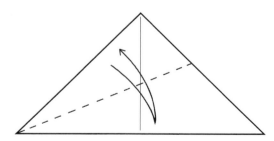

3 Valley fold the top left edge down toward the bottom edge to precrease the paper.

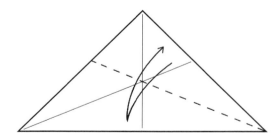

4 Repeat Step 3 on the top right edge.

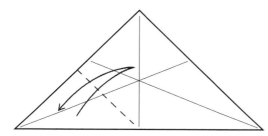

5 Valley fold the left bottom edge toward the creased centerline.

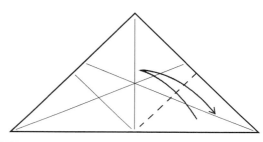

6 Repeat Step 5 on the bottom right-hand edge.

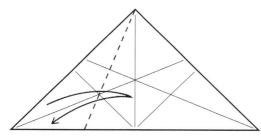

7 Valley fold the top left-hand edge toward the centerline to precrease the paper.

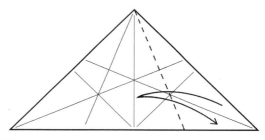

8 Repeat Step 7 on the top right-hand edge.

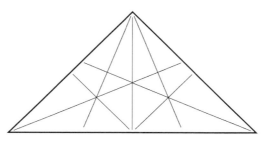

9 All the precreases are completed.

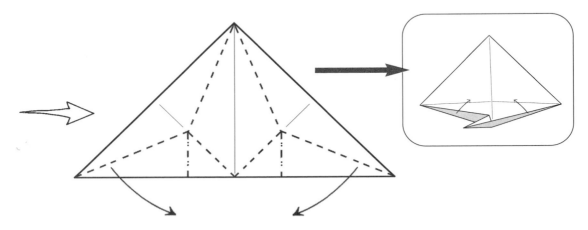

10 Valley fold both left and right edges toward the bottom edge, pulling the corner sections downward to form a rabbit's ear type of folding.

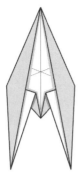

11 Press it flat.

12 Precrease both sides.

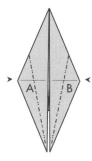

13 Sink in the precreased areas A and B.

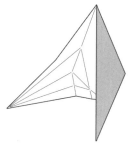

14 Open up the left-hand side, and turn paper sideways.

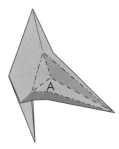

15 Push in the creased section A, and at the same time close the legs back to collapse section A inward until it is completely inverted inside the leg.

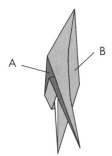

16 Section A is now inverted inside the leg; press it flat to complete the sink.

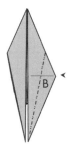

17 Repeat Steps 14 to 16 on side B.

18 Completed Starbase 1.

Starbase 2

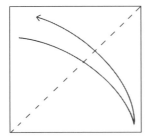

1 Begin with a square piece of paper. Precrease paper at the diagonal line.

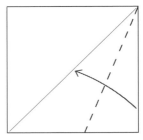

2 Valley fold the right-hand edge toward the diagonal line.

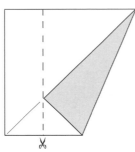

3 Cut paper at the dotted line.

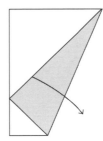

4 Open paper.

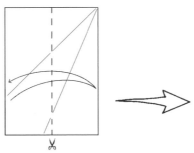

5 Precrease paper in half and cut paper at the halfway line. (This is in fact an "A-sized" paper.)

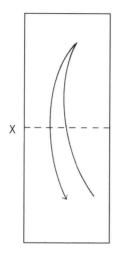

6 Precrease paper in half to mark midpoint X.

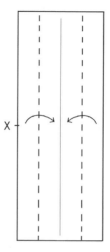

7 Fold sides toward the centerline.

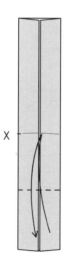

8 Precrease the lower portion halfway to point X (refer to Diagram 6).

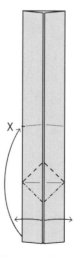

9 Open up the lower half section and fold the bottom edge toward point X.

TIP: Precrease the valley and hill folds to make the step easier.

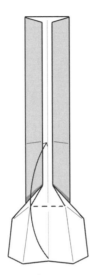

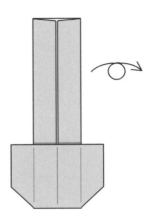

10 Intermediate step—continue to fold upward.

11 Turn over.

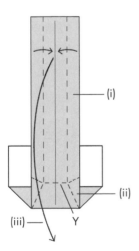

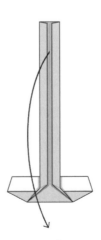

Line Y position

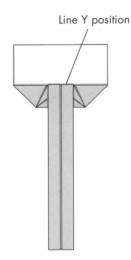

12 (i) Valley fold sides toward centerline, then
(ii) Valley fold the lower part inward, and
(iii) Valley fold the flap downward at line Y.

TIP: Precrease line Y to make this step easier.

13 Intermediate step—continue to fold downward.

14 Completed Starbase 2.

FEDERATION VESSELS

U.S.S. Enterprise™ NCC-1701

A two-piece model. Begin with Starbase 1.

Starbase 1

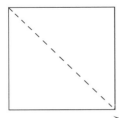

1a Begin with a square piece of paper. Make a diagonal crease and cut at dotted line to create two isosceles triangles.

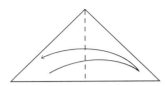

2a Take one of the triangles and precrease at the centerline. (Keep the other triangle; it will be used to fold the saucer section of the ship.)

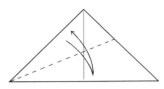

3a Valley fold the top left edge down toward the bottom edge to precrease the paper.

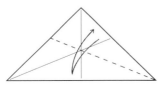

4a Repeat Step 3 on the top right edge.

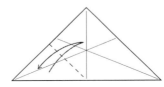

5a Valley fold the left bottom edge toward the creased centerline.

6a Repeat Step 5 on the bottom right-hand edge.

7a Valley fold the top left-hand edge toward the centerline to precrease the paper.

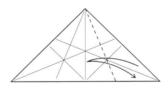

8a Repeat Step 7 on the top right-hand edge.

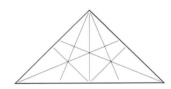

9a All the precreases are completed.

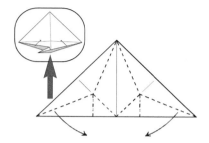

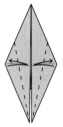

10a Valley fold both left and right edges toward the bottom edge, pulling the corner sections downward to form a rabbit's ear type of folding.

11a Press it flat.

12a Precrease both sides.

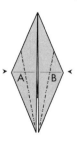

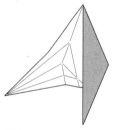

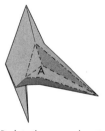

13a Sink in the precreased areas A and B.

14a Open up the left-hand side, and turn paper sideways.

15a Push in the creased section A, and at the same time close the legs back to collapse section A inward until it is completely inverted inside the leg.

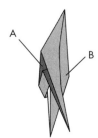

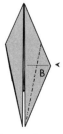

16a Section A is now inverted inside the leg; press it flat to complete the sink.

17a Repeat Steps 14 to 16 on side B.

18a Completed Starbase 1.

Engineering Section

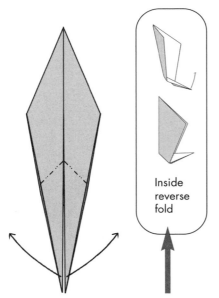

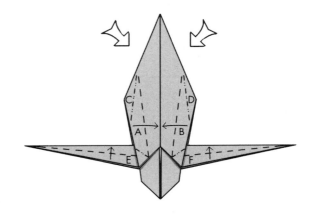

1 Inside reverse fold both legs upward.

2 Fold top layers A and B toward center, squashing flat areas C and D and pulling up flaps E and F simultaneously.

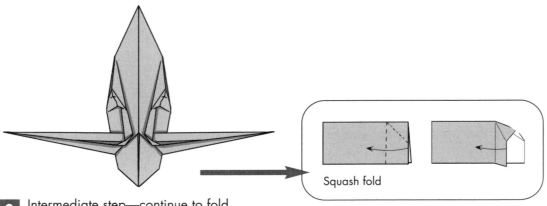

3 Intermediate step—continue to fold toward center.

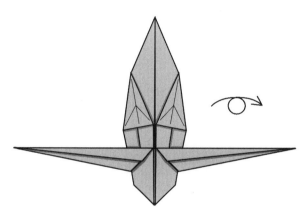

4 Turn over.

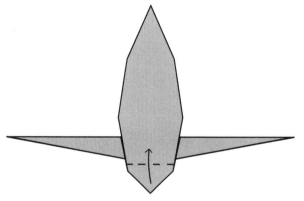

5 Valley fold lower section upward.

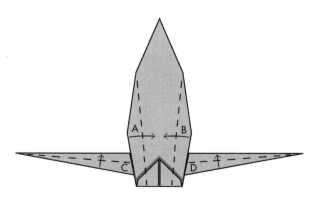

6 Valley fold sides A and B toward center and pull up flaps C and D simultaneously.

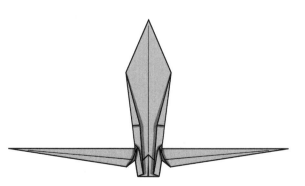

7 Intermediate step—continue to fold toward center.

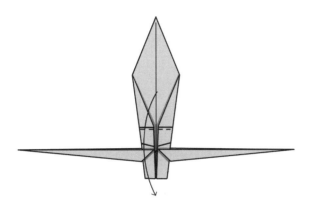

8 Valley fold flap down.

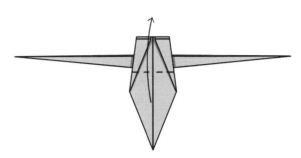

9 Valley fold flap back up.

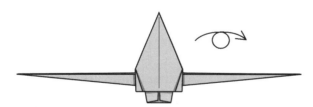

10 Turn over.

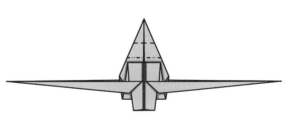

11 Follow the lines for a zigzag fold.

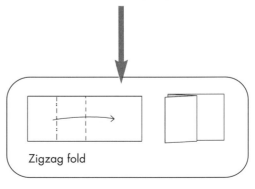

Zigzag fold

12 Turn over.
The following is an enlarged diagram.

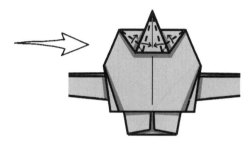

13 Fold as indicated to narrow the tip section.

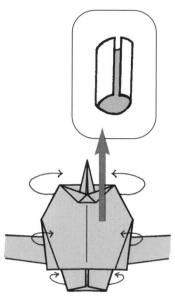

14 Roll the entire section into a cylindrical shape.

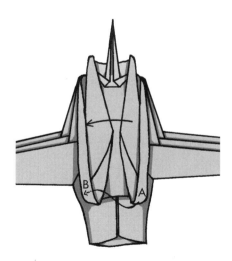

15 Insert section A into pocket B.

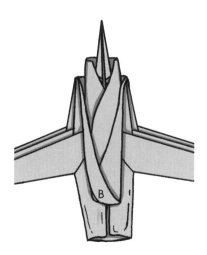

16 Re-enforce the fold by squeezing the flaps together slightly.

SIDE PROFILE

17 Pull across the upper layer of the arm and press flat.

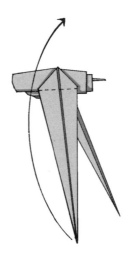

18 Fold arm upward.

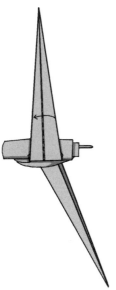

19 Close up arm.

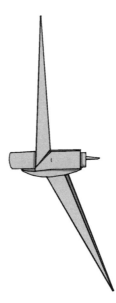

20 Repeat Steps 17 to 29 on the other arm.

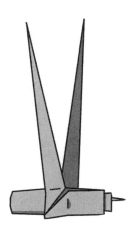

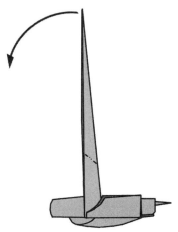

21 Follow the next steps carefully for the nacelle section.

22 Inside reverse fold arm downward.

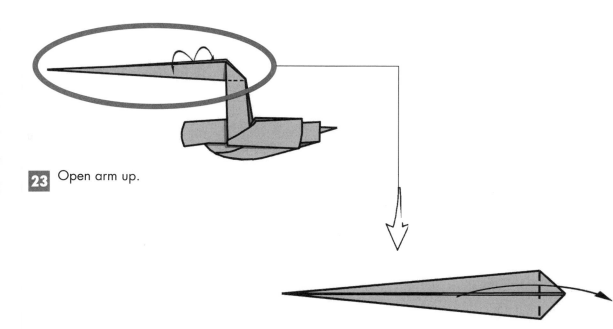

23 Open arm up.

24 Enlarged top down view—fold up arm.

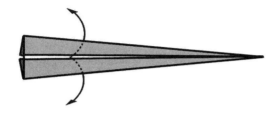

25 Open up bottom flaps completely and press flat.

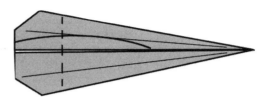

26 Fold arm as indicated.

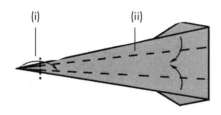

27 (i) Fold the tip corner inward.
(ii) Fold sides toward center, and

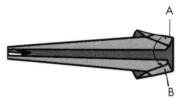

28 Insert flap A underneath flap B.

29 Re-enforce the fold by squeezing the flaps together slightly.

Saucer Section

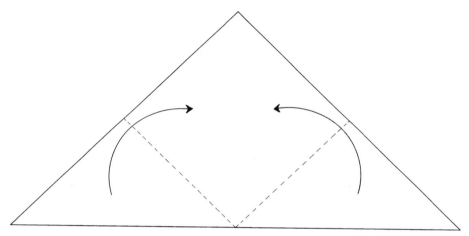

30 Begin with the other triangle cut out from the square paper. Fold both corners upward toward center.

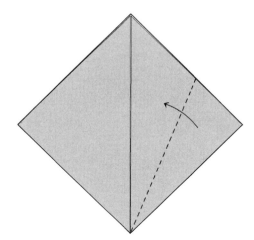

31 Valley fold across.

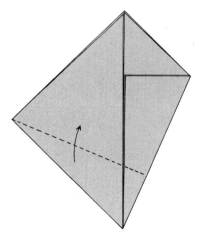

32 Valley fold upward.

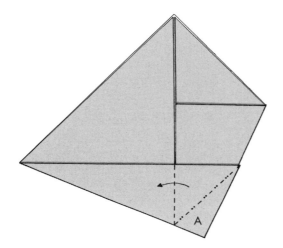

33 Fold flap across and squash open area A.

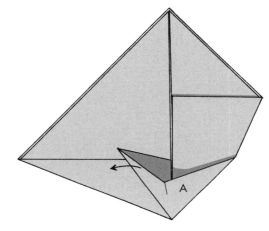

34 Intermediate step.

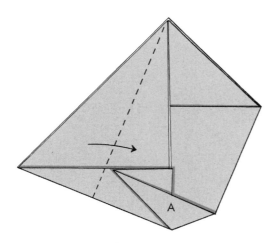

35 Repeat steps as follows.

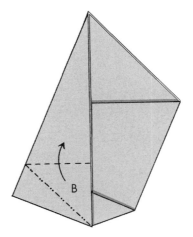

36 Fold across and squash open area B.

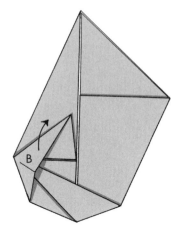

37 Intermediate step.

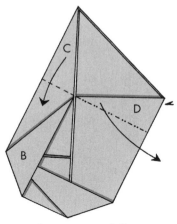

38 Repeat similar steps as follows.
  (i) Slowly pull open flap D and fold area
      C across, and
  (ii) Reverse/sink area D inside simultaneously.

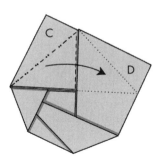

39 Fold across and squash open area C.

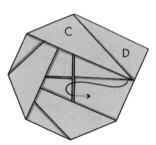

40 Insert flap C underneath flap D.

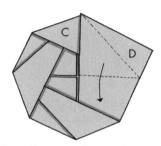

41 Fold flap down and squash open area D.

42 Fold section D upward.

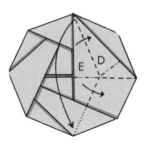

43 Fold area E across, pulling down section D simultaneously.

44 Intermediate step—continue to valley fold section E across and gently valley fold D downward.

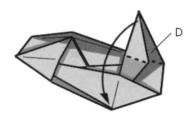

45 Intermediate step—E is now folded completely across. Valley fold arm D flat.

46 Lift arm up to a vertical position.

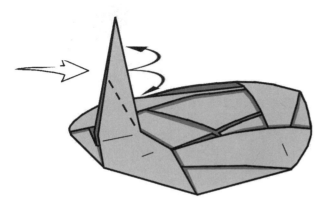

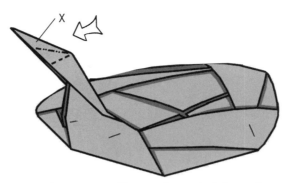

47 Side view—outside reverse arm outward.
TIP: Precreasing the arm will make this step easier and more accurate.

48 Side view—pull open flaps slightly and press section X open.

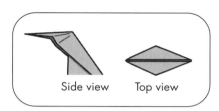

Side view   Top view

 Section X

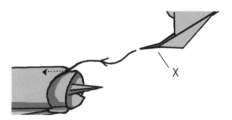

X

50 Insert section X of the saucer section into the gap located on top of the deflector dish at the ship's engineering section.

U.S.S. Enterprise NCC-1701

U.S.S. Enterprise™ NCC-1701-A

A two piece model, begin with Starbase 1.

Starbase 1

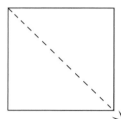

1a Begin with a square piece of paper. Make a diagonal crease and cut at dotted line to create two isosceles triangles.

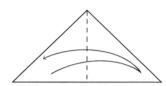

2a Take one of the triangles and precrease at the centerline. (Keep the other triangle; it will be used to fold the saucer section of the ship.)

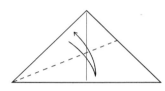

3a Valley fold the top left edge down toward the bottom edge to precrease the paper.

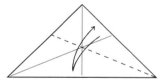

4a Repeat Step 3 on the top right edge.

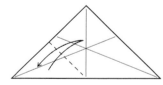

5a Valley fold the left bottom edge toward the creased centerline.

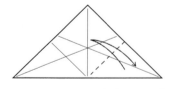

6a Repeat Step 5 on the bottom right-hand edge.

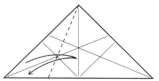

7a Valley fold the top left-hand edge toward the centerline to precrease the paper.

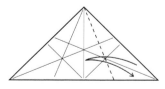

8a Repeat Step 7 on the top right-hand edge.

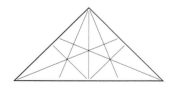

9a All the precreases are completed.

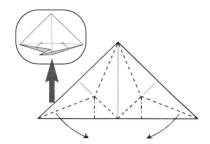

10a Valley fold both left and right edges toward the bottom edge, pulling the corner sections downward to form a rabbit's ear type of folding.

11a Press it flat.

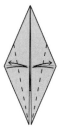

12a Precrease both sides.

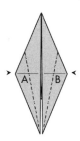

13a Sink in the precreased areas A and B.

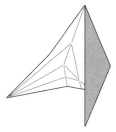

14a Open up the left-hand side, and turn paper sideways.

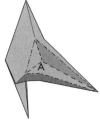

15a Push in the creased section A, and at the same time close the legs back to collapse section A inward until it is completely inverted inside the leg.

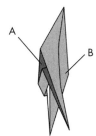

16a Section A is now inverted inside the leg; press it flat to complete the sink.

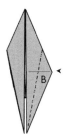

17a Repeat Steps 14 to 16 on side B.

18a Completed Starbase 1.

Engineering Section

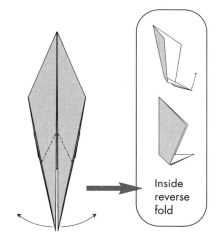

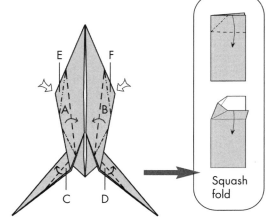

Inside reverse fold

1   Inside reverse fold legs outward.

2   Fold areas A and B toward center, squashing flat areas E and F and pulling up flaps C and D simultaneously.

Squash fold

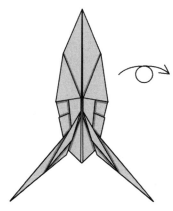

3   Turn over.

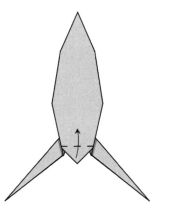

4   Valley fold lower flap upward.

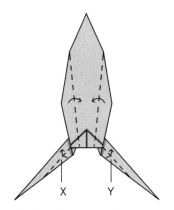

5 Valley fold sides toward center and pull up flaps X and Y simultaneously.

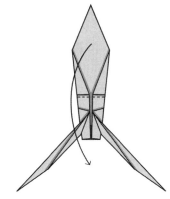

6 Valley fold flap down.

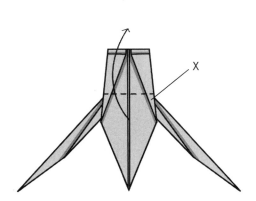

7 Valley fold flap back up.

TIP: The fold up position is located just above the cross section position X.

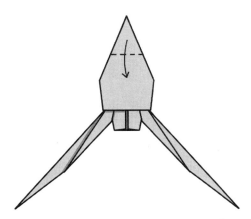

8 Valley fold the small tip section down.

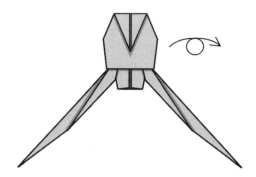

9 Turn over to review the opposite side.

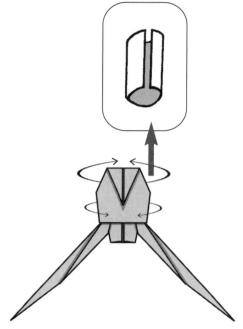

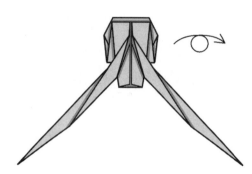

10 This side should look like this; turn back over for the next step.

11 Roll the main body section into a cylindrical shape.

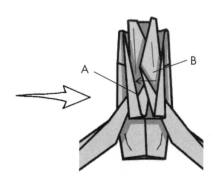

12 Insert flap B into pocket A.

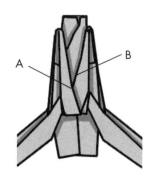

13 Re-enforce the fold by squashing the flaps together slightly.

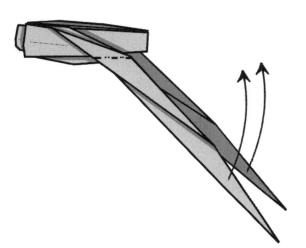

14 Inside reverse fold both wings upward.

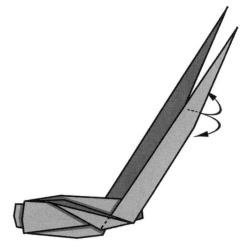

15 Open up both flaps.

16 Fold sides toward the middle.

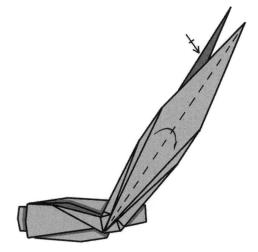

17 Close flaps back, and repeat Steps 15 to 17 on the other wing.

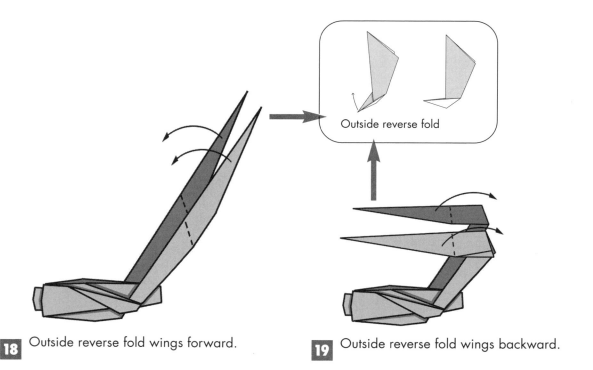

Outside reverse fold

18 Outside reverse fold wings forward.

19 Outside reverse fold wings backward.

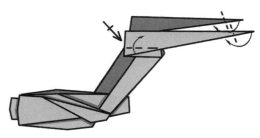

20 (i) Fold the smaller lower corners on each of the nacelles upward.
(ii) Fold inward the end tip sections on both nacelles.

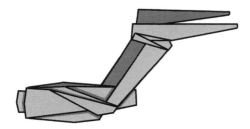

21 Completed engineering section.

Saucer Section

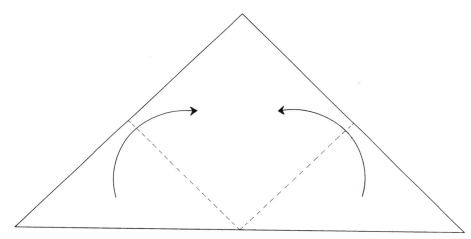

22 Begin with the other triangle cut out from the square paper. Fold both corners upward toward center.

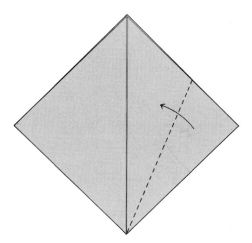

23 Valley fold across.

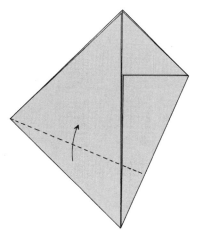

24 Valley fold upward.

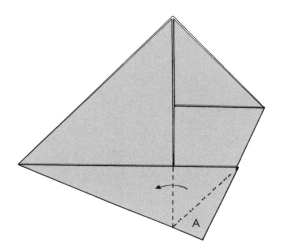

25 Fold flap across and squash open area A.

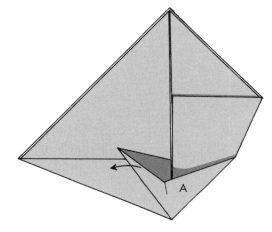

26 Intermediate step.

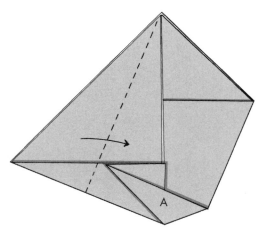

27 Repeat steps as follows.

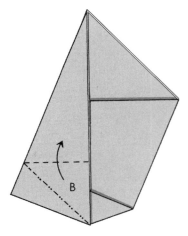

28 Fold across and squash open area B.

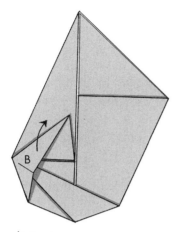

29 Intermediate step.

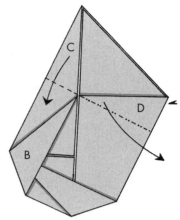

30 Repeat similar steps as follows.
(i) Slowly pull open flap D and fold area C across, and
(ii) Reverse/sink area D inside simultaneously.

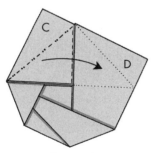

31 Fold across and squash open area C.

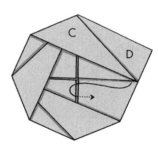

32 Insert flap C underneath flap D.

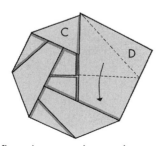

33 Fold flap down and squash open area D.

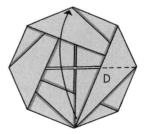

34 Fold section D upward.

35 Fold area E across, and pull down section D simultaneously.

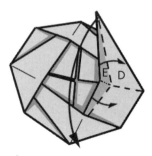

36 Intermediate step—continue to valley fold section E across and gently valley fold D downward.

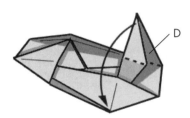

37 Intermediate step—E is now folded completely across. Valley fold arm D flat.

38 Lift arm up to a vertical position.

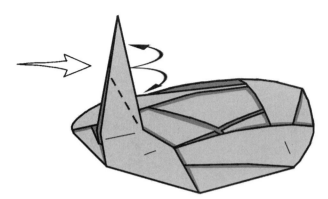

39 Side view—outside reverse arm outward.

TIP: Precreasing the arm will make this step easier and more accurate.

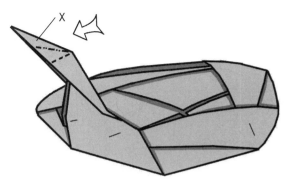

40 Side view—pull open flaps slightly and press section X open.

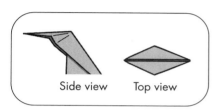

41 Section X

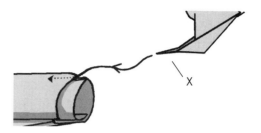

42 Insert section X of the saucer section into the gap located on top of the deflector dish at the ship's engineering section.

U.S.S. Enterprise NCC-1701-A

U.S.S. Enterprise™ NCC-1701-D

Begin with Starbase 2.

Starbase 2

1a Begin with a square piece of paper. Precrease paper at the diagonal line.

2a Valley fold the right-hand edge toward the diagonal line.

3a Cut paper at the dotted line.

4a Open paper.

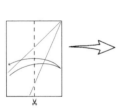
5a Precrease paper in half and cut paper at the halfway line. (This is in fact an "A-sized" paper.)

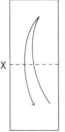
6a Precrease paper in half to mark midpoint X.

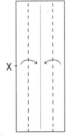
7a Fold sides toward the centerline.

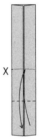
8a Precrease the paper halfway to point X (refer to Diagram 6).

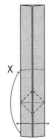
9a Open up the lower half section and fold the bottom edge toward point X.

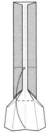
10a Intermediate step—continue to fold upward.

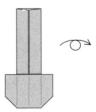
11a Turn over.

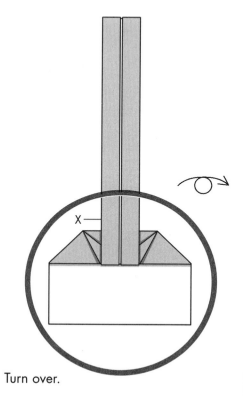

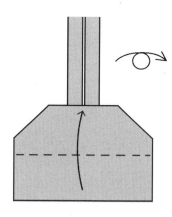

1 Turn over.

2 Valley fold the bottom edge up toward the top edge and turn over.

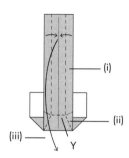

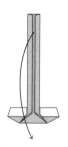

Line Y position

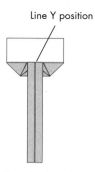

12a (i) Valley fold sides toward centerline, then (ii) Valley fold the lower part inward, and (iii) Valley fold the flap downward at line Y.

13a Intermediate step— continue to fold downward.

14a Completed Starbase 2.

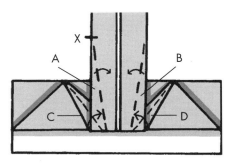

3 Note point X (Diagram 1).
Fold sections A and B inward, pulling up
sections C and D simultaneously.

*TIP: Sections C and D will be pulled and
valley folded upward; this part may get
bulky.*

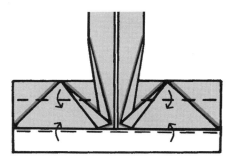

4 Valley fold as indicated.

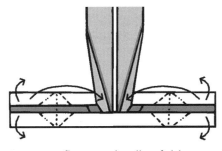

5 Open up flaps and valley fold toward center.

*TIP: Precreasing the hill and valley folds makes
this step easier and more accurate.*

*TIP: Similar fold to Steps 3 through 5 of
Starbase 2.*

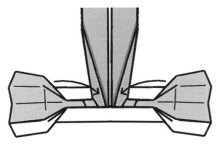

6 Intermediate step—continue to fold toward
center.

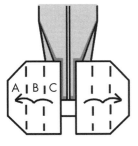

7 Fold A to B and then to C.

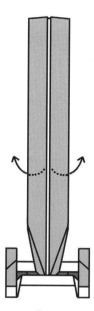

8 Open up bottom flaps.

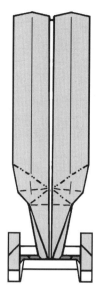

9 Follow the hill and valley lines carefully to form a small hill section before folding downward.

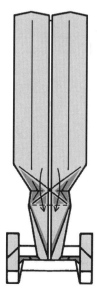

10 Intermediate step—slowly flatten the fold by pulling the small hill section downward.

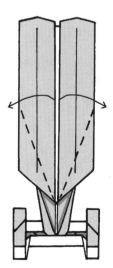

11 Open up the two front flaps, and

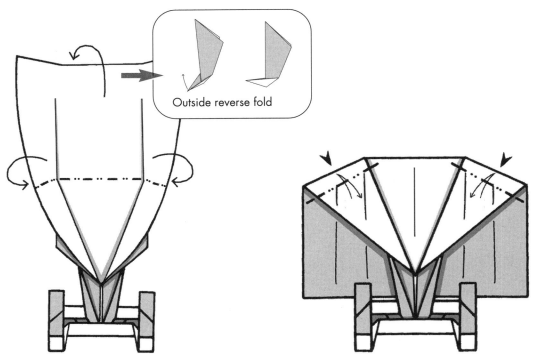

Outside reverse fold

12 Carefully flip and outside reverse fold the entire two opened flaps backward. (Check the next diagram.)

13 Precrease and inside reverse fold the two top corner sections.

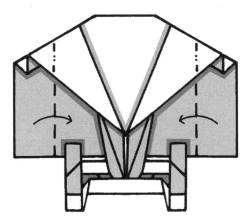

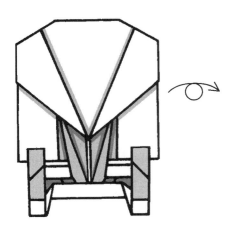

14 Inside reverse fold the two side sections.

15 Turn over.

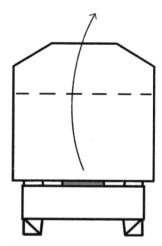

16 Valley fold flap upward.

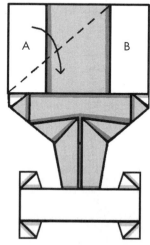

17 Valley fold corner A down.

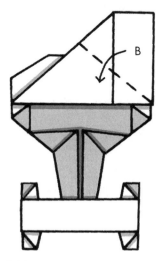

18 Valley fold corner B down.

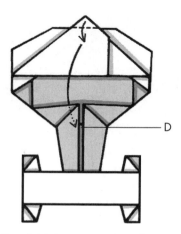

19 (i) Valley fold the tip section down, and
(ii) Valley fold the entire triangular flap into pocket D.

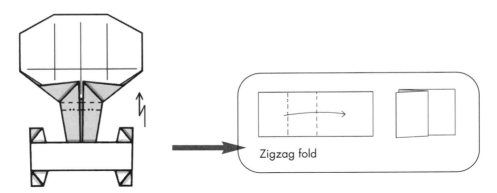

Zigzag fold

20 Follow the lines for a zigzag fold.

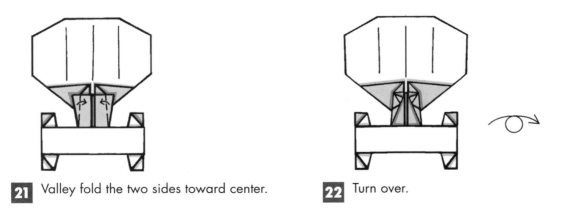

21 Valley fold the two sides toward center.

22 Turn over.

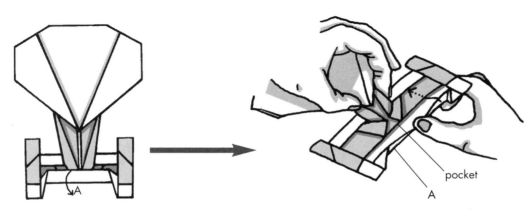

pocket

A

23 Pull down flap A and slip the entire section into the pocket located underneath.

24 Slightly curve this section up (both sides).

25 Slightly bend both nacelle sections outward.

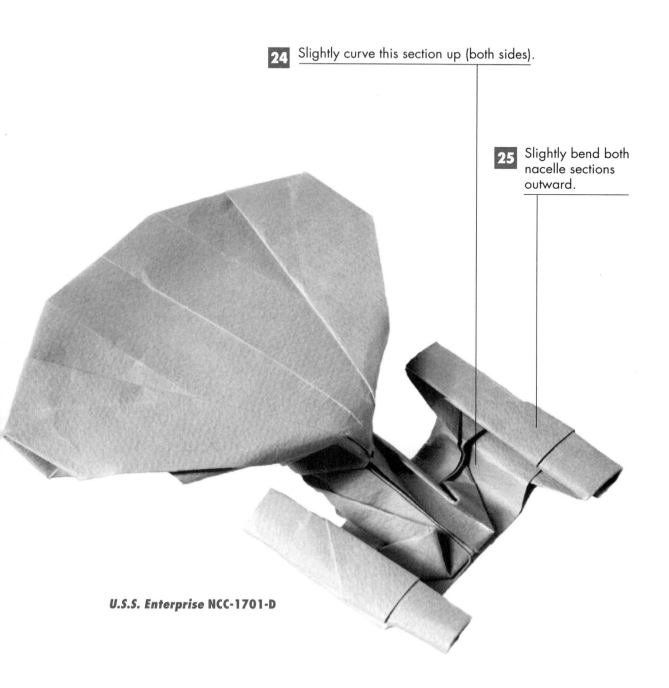

U.S.S. Enterprise NCC-1701-D

U.S.S. Enterprise™ NCC-1701-E

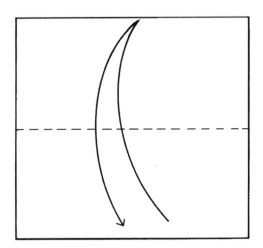

1 Begin with a square piece of paper. Precrease paper in half.

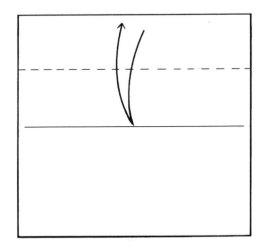

2 Precrease paper in quarter.

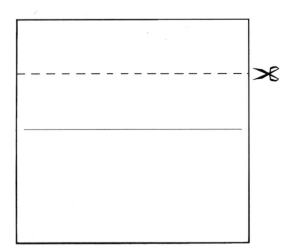

3 Cut paper at the dotted line.

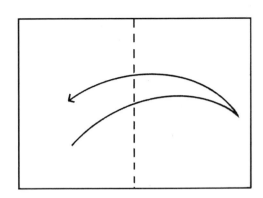

4 Precrease paper in half horizontally.

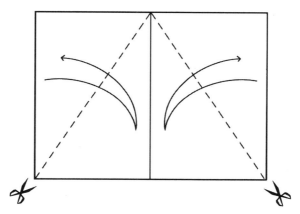

5 Precrease and cut paper on the dotted lines.

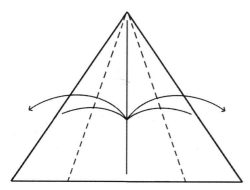

6 Precrease the two sides toward the center.

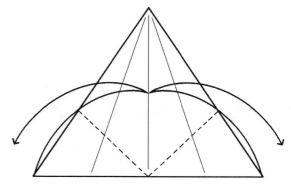

7 Precrease the two bottom edges toward the centerline.

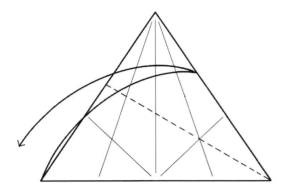

8 Precrease the left-hand edge toward the bottom edge and repeat the same step on the right-hand side.

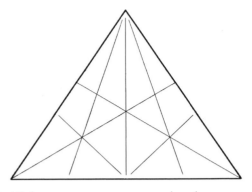

9 All the precreases are completed.

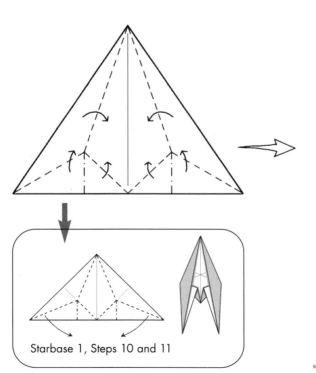

Starbase 1, Steps 10 and 11

10 Follow the lines and arrows to form a rabbit's ear type of fold (similar to Steps 10 and 11 of Starbase 1).

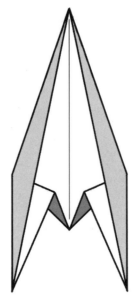

11 Intermediate step.

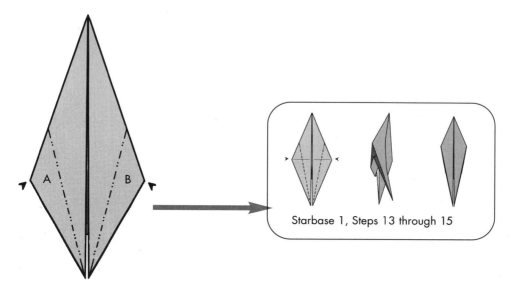

Starbase 1, Steps 13 through 15

12 Sink in areas A and B (similar to Steps 13 through 15 of Starbase 1).

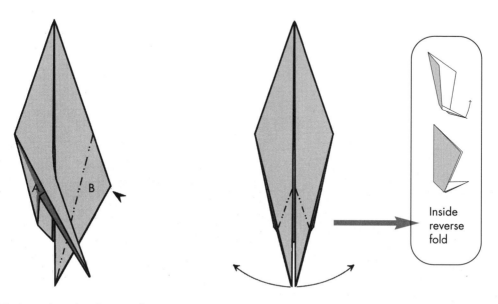

Inside reverse fold

13 Completed sink on side A. Repeat on area B.

14 Inside reverse fold both legs upward.
TIP: All folds should be precise or it will be slightly difficult to make an inside reverse fold.

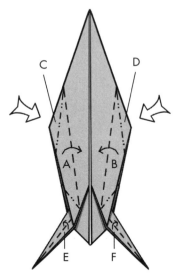

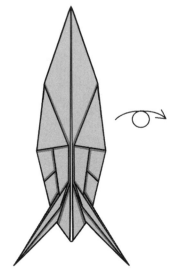

15 Fold areas A and B toward the center, pulling up areas E and F and squashing flat areas C and D simultaneously.

16 Turn over.

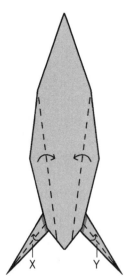

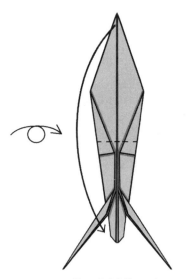

17 Valley fold sides toward the center, pulling up areas X and Y simultaneously, before turning over to the other side.

18 Valley fold flap down.

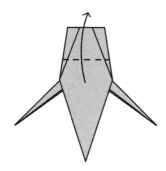

19 Valley fold flap up.

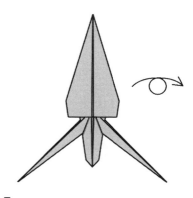

20 Turn over.

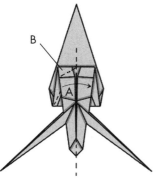

21 Valley fold side A across and squash open area B.

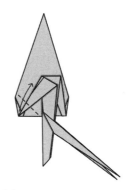

22 Valley fold corner section up.

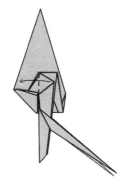

23 Fold flap back across.

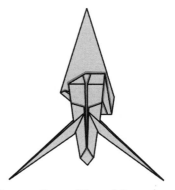

24 Repeat Steps 21 to 23 on the right-hand side.

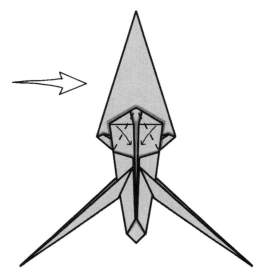

25 Valley fold both sections down toward the center.

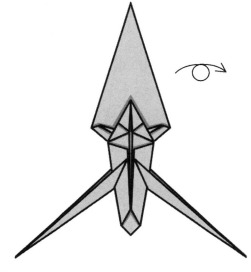

26 Turn over.

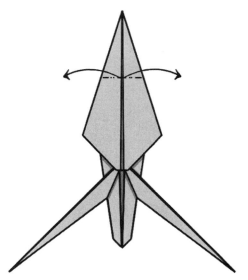

27 Open the top layer flaps and reverse fold in the top section.

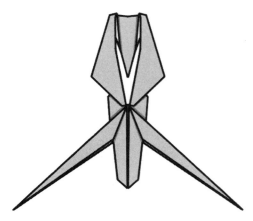

28 Intermediate step—close flaps back.

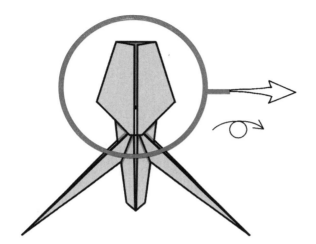

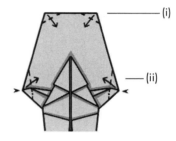

29 Turn over. The following is an enlarged saucer section.

30 (i) Valley fold top two corners down.
(ii) Inside reverse fold inward the two small side sections.

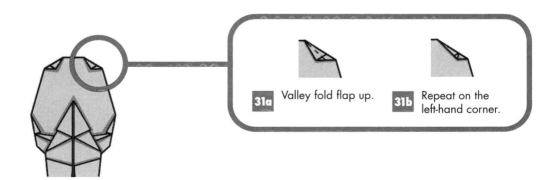

31a Valley fold flap up.

31b Repeat on the left-hand corner.

31 The following are enlarged top corner sections.

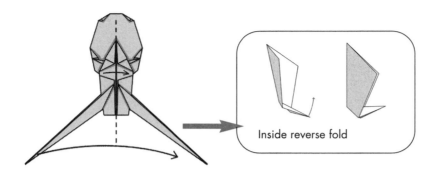

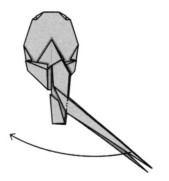

Inside reverse fold

32 Fold the entire left upper layer across.

33 Inside reverse fold wing back across.

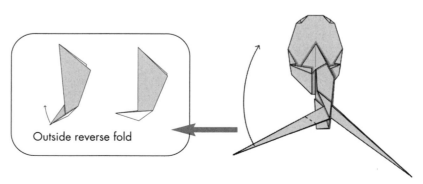

Outside reverse fold

34 Outside reverse fold wing up.

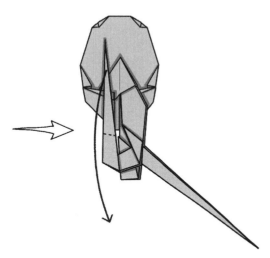

35 Outside reverse fold wing down.

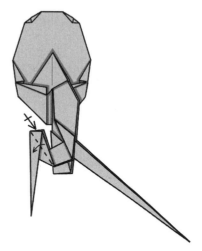

36 Valley fold wing section as indicated, and repeat the step on the other side.

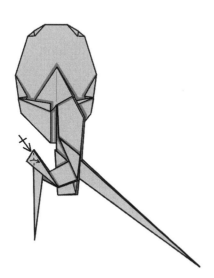

37 Valley fold the small tip section back across, and repeat step on the other side.

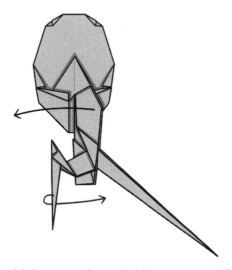

38 Fold the upper layer back across, and flip the nacelle section behind.

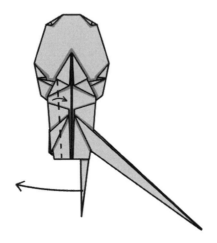

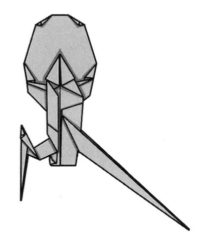

39 Valley fold to narrow the main body section, and flip the nacelle section back across.

40 Repeat Steps 32 to 39 on the right-hand side.

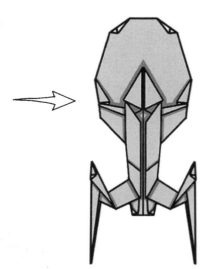

Finished Diagram—Ventral View.

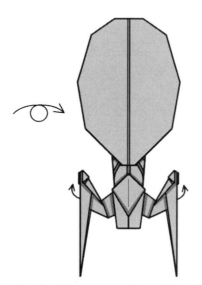

41 Finished Diagram—Dorsal View. (Curve up both wing sections.)

Finished Diagram—Side Profile.

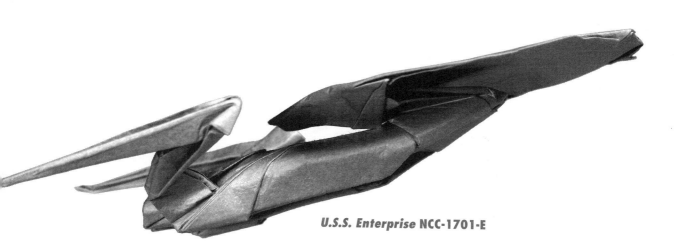

U.S.S. Enterprise NCC-1701-E

U.S.S. Defiant NX-74205

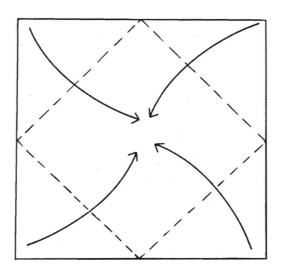

1 Begin with a square piece of paper. Fold all four corners toward center.

TIP: Precrease the paper halfway across both vertically and horizontally to locate the middle point.

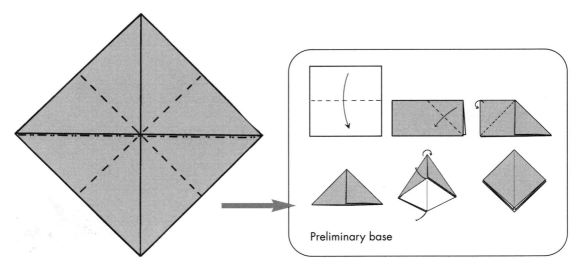

Preliminary base

2 Using the resulting square as a base, fold it into a preliminary base.

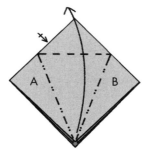

3 Intermediate step—preliminary base, continue to fold into a bird base by lifting up the front flap and gently valley fold in areas A and B toward center.

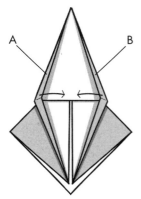

4 Intermediate step—continue to push in areas A and B toward center.

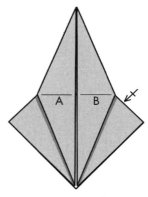

5 Turn over, repeat Steps 3 through 5 on the other side.

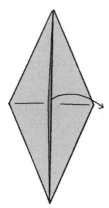

6 Pull open the front right flap to reveal the inside layer.

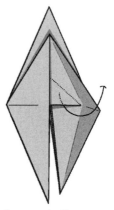

7 Slowly pull the inside flap out completely.

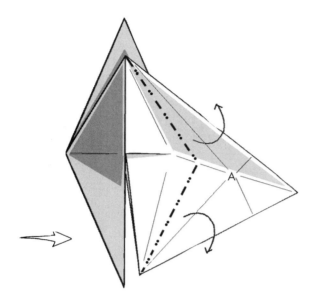

8 Reverse and flip the entire section A outward.

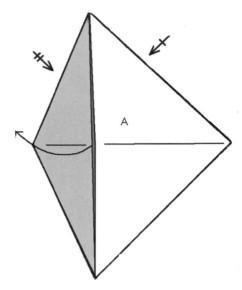

9 Repeat Steps 6 through 9 on the left-hand side and on the two flaps behind as well.

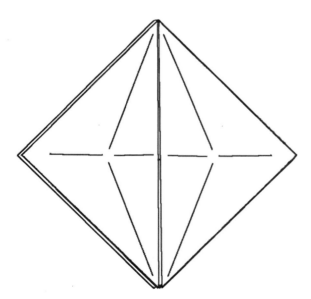

10 All four flaps are pulled out.

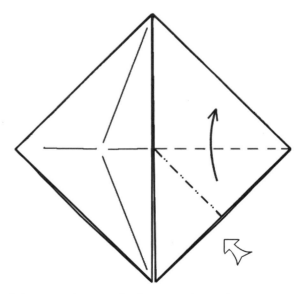

11 Squash open the lower right pocket.

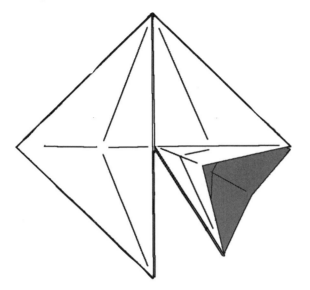

12 Intermediate step—push pocket upward.

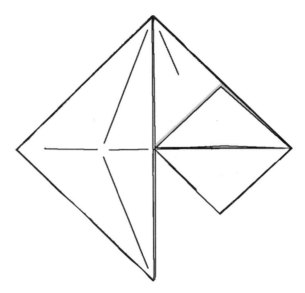

13 Repeat Steps 11 and 12 on the left-hand side.

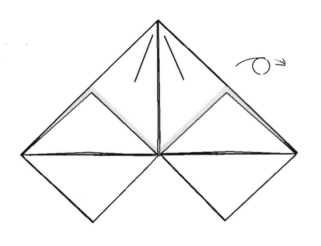

14 Turn over.

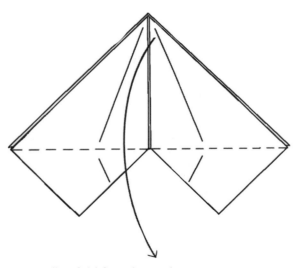

15 Valley fold front layer down.

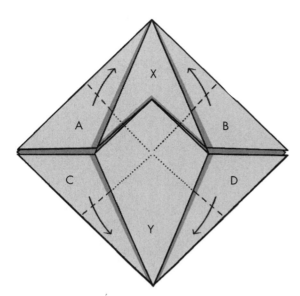

16

(i) Lift up flap A to valley fold underneath flap X, and

(ii) Similarly lift up flap B to valley fold underneath flap X.

(iii) Lift up flap C to valley fold underneath flap Y.

(iv) Similarly lift up flap D to valley fold underneath flap Y.

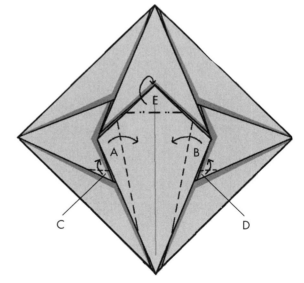

17

(i) Valley fold areas A and B inward.

TIP: Note that areas C and D will be pulled and valley folded upward toward the front.

(ii) Hill fold area E behind.

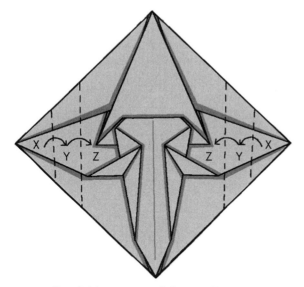

18 Valley fold X to Y and then to Z.

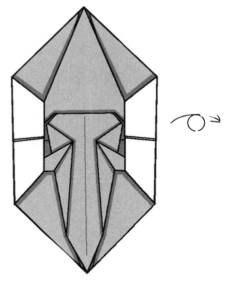

19 Turn over.

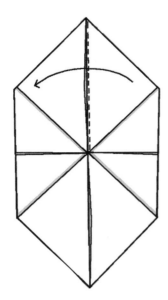

20 Valley fold the upper flap across.

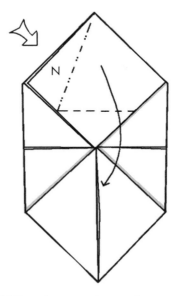

21 Fold flap down and squash open section N.
TIP: Precrease valley and hill fold, as shown.

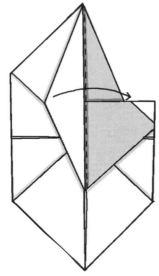

22 Fold flap back across.

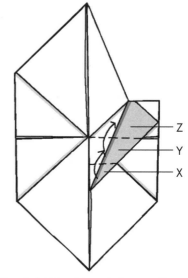

23 Valley fold X to Y and then to Z.

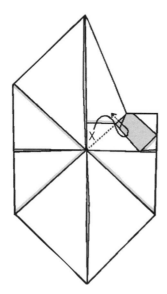

24 Insert flap X into the pocket underneath.

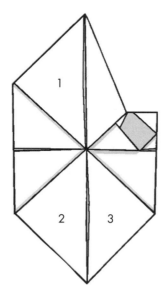

25 Repeat Steps 18 through 22 on sections 1, 2, and 3.

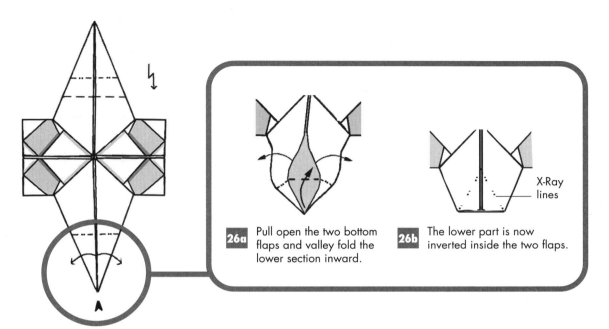

26a Pull open the two bottom flaps and valley fold the lower section inward.

26b The lower part is now inverted inside the two flaps.

X-Ray lines

26 Zigzag fold the upper section.

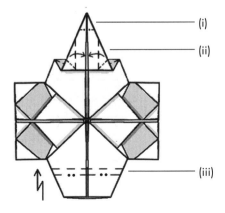

(i)

(ii)

(iii)

27 (i) Pull open the two upper flaps and valley fold inward the tip section (similar to 26a).
(ii) Valley fold the two sides inward to narrow the tip section.
(iii) Zigzag fold the lower section.

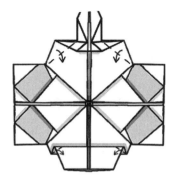

28 Valley fold the two upper corners and the two lower corners to complete the fold.

Ventral View

U.S.S. Defiant NX-74205

U.S.S. Voyager™ NCC-74656

Begin with Step 6 of Starbase 2.

Starbase 2

1a Begin with a square piece of paper. Precrease paper at the diagonal line.

2a Valley fold the right-hand edge toward the diagonal line.

3a Cut paper at the dotted line.

4a Open paper.

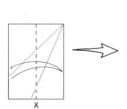

5a Precrease paper in half and cut paper at the halfway line. (This is in fact an "A-sized" paper.)

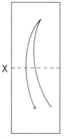

6a Precrease paper in half to mark midpoint X.

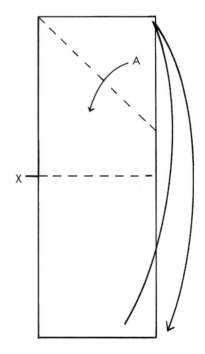

(i) Valley fold area A downward.
(ii) Precrease paper halfway to mark vertical midpoint X.

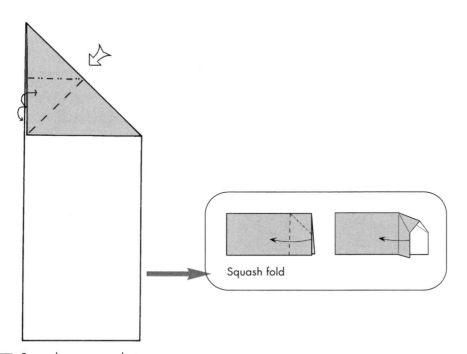

Squash fold

2 Squash open pocket.
TIP: Precrease hill and valley fold, as shown, and then squash.+-

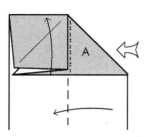

3 Valley fold flap across and reverse fold triangular section A inward.

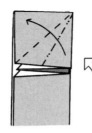

4 Lift out top flap and squash open pocket.

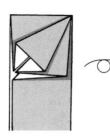

5 Turn over.

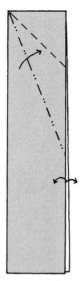

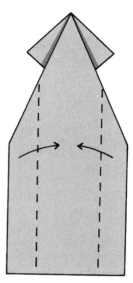

6

Pull open flaps and squash them open.
Check the finished step in Diagram 7

*TIP: Precrease hill and valley fold, as shown.
When opening up flaps, hold onto the top square
area and then squash open flap as indicated.*

7 Valley fold sides toward the
centerline.

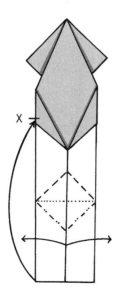

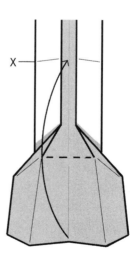

8

Pull open flaps and valley fold bottom edge to midpoint
X (similar to Steps 3 through 5 of Starbase 2).

TIP: Precrease hill and valley folds, as shown.

9 Intermediate step.

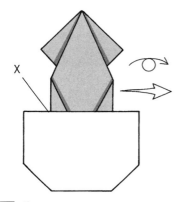

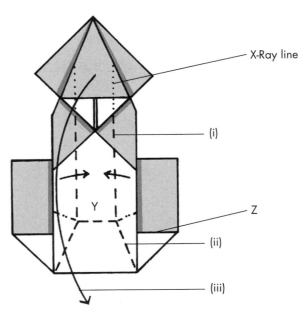

X-Ray line

(i)

Y

Z

(ii)

(iii)

X

10 Turn over.

11 Valley fold both sides toward center, and

TIP: Similar to Step 12 of Starbase 2. The sides should be folded underneath the top triangular section. Do not fold the triangular section.

(ii) Valley fold the lower part inward, and
(iii) Valley fold the entire upper flap downward at line Y.

TIP: Y is slightly above line Z.

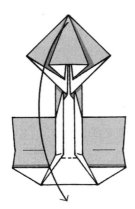

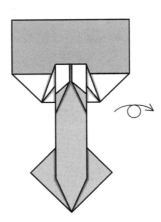

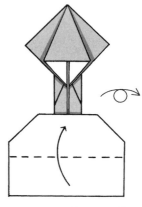

12 Intermediate step—continuing to fold downward.

13 Turn over and rotate paper back upright.

14 Valley fold bottom flap upward and turn over.

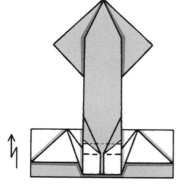

15 Follow the lines for a zigzag fold.

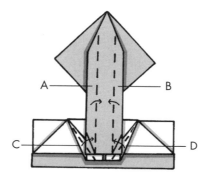

16 Fold sides A and B toward center, and pull up areas C and D simultaneously.

TIP: Sections C and D will be pulled and valley folded upward. This part may get slightly bulky.

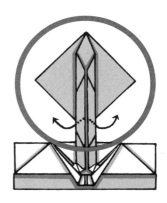

17 Pull open flaps located below for the next three steps.

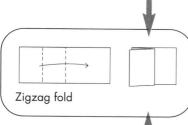

Zigzag fold

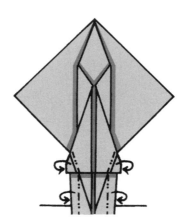

18 Follow the lines for a zigzag fold.

19 Hill fold sides back behind to close flaps back.

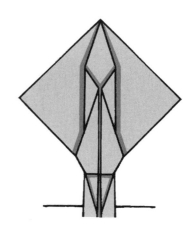

20 Finished folds.

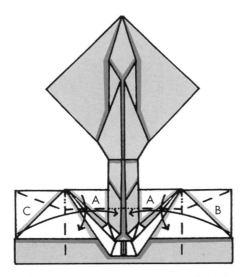

21 Valley fold section A downward while pulling across section B and C simultaneously.

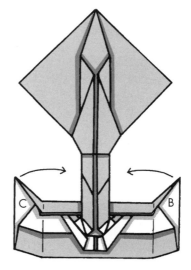

22 Intermediate step.

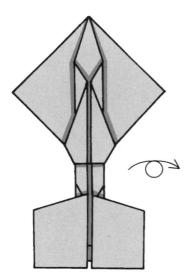

23 Turn over.

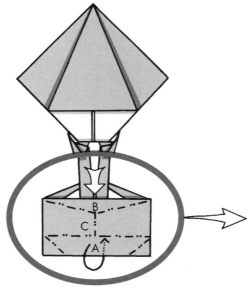

24 (i) Hill fold bottom section A into the pocket underneath.
(ii) Push area B in to form a small hill at section C.

Engineering Section

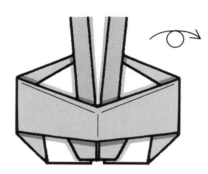

25 Turn over.

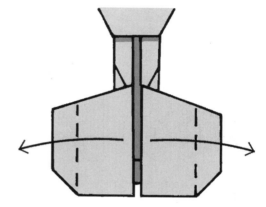

26 Valley fold flaps outward.

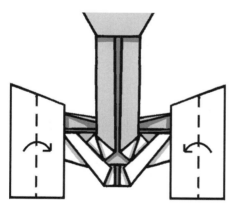

27 Valley fold flaps inward.

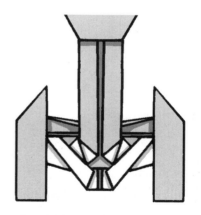

28 Completed *Voyager*'s engineering section.

Saucer Section

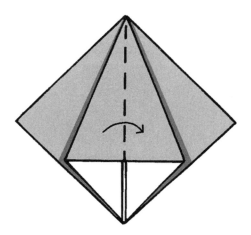

29 Valley fold top flap across.

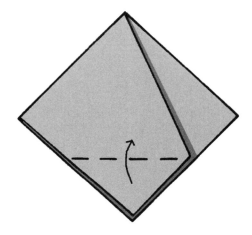

30 Valley fold bottom flap upward.

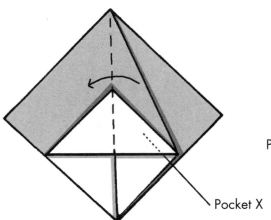

Pocket X

31 Valley fold flap back across.

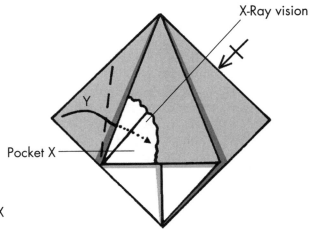

X-Ray vision

Y

Pocket X

32 (i) Valley fold section Y into pocket X.
(ii) Repeat on the right-hand side.

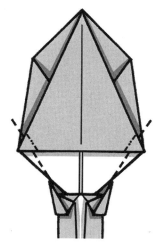

33 Valley fold the lower layer while reverse folding inward the upper triangular section.

34 Inflate pocket slightly to complete *Voyager's* saucer section.

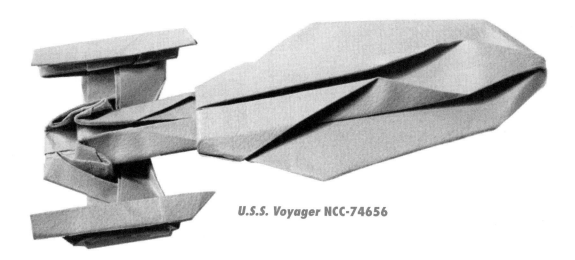

U.S.S. Voyager NCC-74656

Shuttlecraft Type-6

As seen in Star Trek: The Next Generation.

Begin with Step 6 of Starbase 2.

Starbase 2

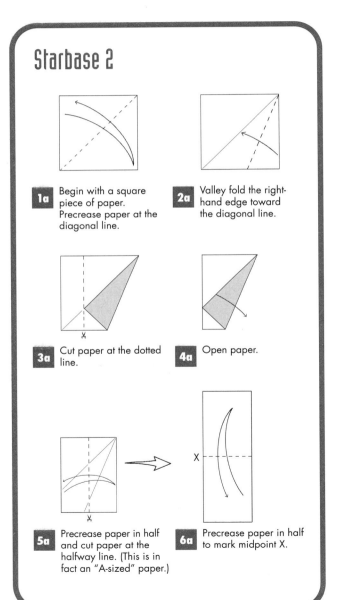

1a Begin with a square piece of paper. Precrease paper at the diagonal line.

2a Valley fold the right-hand edge toward the diagonal line.

3a Cut paper at the dotted line.

4a Open paper.

5a Precrease paper in half and cut paper at the halfway line. (This is in fact an "A-sized" paper.)

6a Precrease paper in half to mark midpoint X.

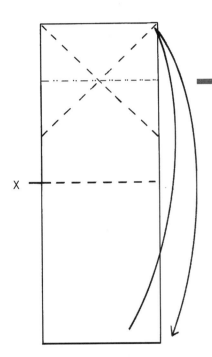

1
(i) Fold and unfold to mark vertical midpoint X.
(ii) Fold the top section into a water bomb base.

Water Bomb Base

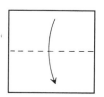

1b Begin with a square piece of paper. Valley fold paper in half.

2b Pull across the upper layer from the halfway line and squash open pocket.

TIP: Precrease valley fold and hill fold before folding across.

3b Turn over and repeat on the other side.

TIP: As in Step 2, precrease the paper prior to the actual fold.

4b Squash flat to complete a water bomb base.

5b Completed water bomb base.

2 Fold top flap A across.

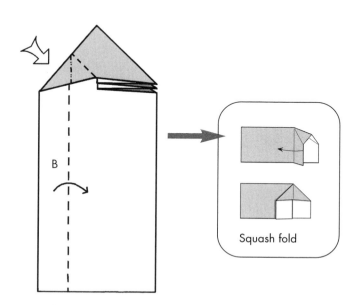

3 Valley fold flap B across and squash open top section simultaneously.

Squash fold

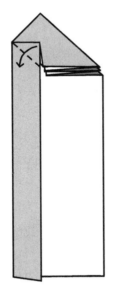

4 Fold corner section downward.

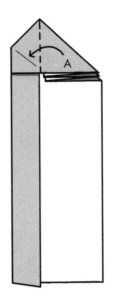

5 Fold flap A back across.

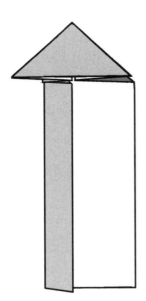

6 Repeat Steps 2 to 5 on the right-hand side.

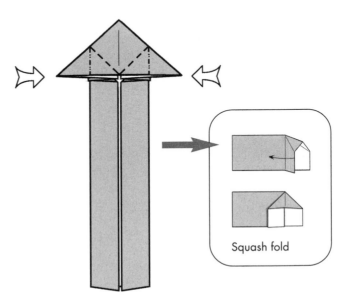

Squash fold

7 Squash open both pockets.

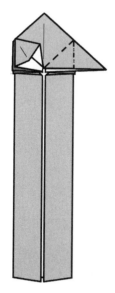

8 Intermediate step.

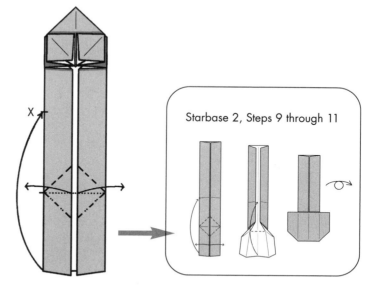

Starbase 2, Steps 9 through 11

9 Open flaps and fold the bottom edge toward point X in diagram 1 (similar to Steps 9 to 11 of Starbase 2).

TIP: Precrease hill and valley fold, as shown.

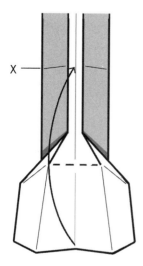

10 Intermediate step—continue to fold upward.

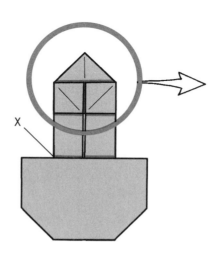

11 See enlarged diagram of top section.

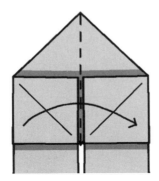

12 Fold the top left-hand flap across.

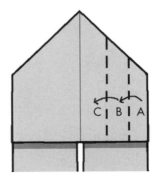

13 Valley fold A to B and then to C.

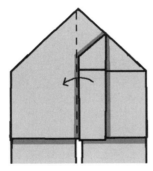

14 Fold flap back across.

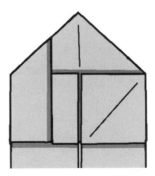

15 Repeat Steps 11 to 13 on right-hand side.

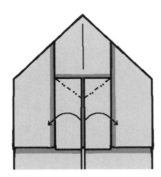

16 Pull flaps open and squash open the two corners.

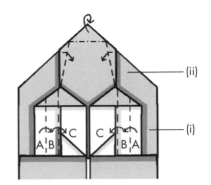

17 (i) Valley fold areas A to B and then to C on both sides.
(ii) Hill fold the top corners behind and valley fold the two side sections inward.

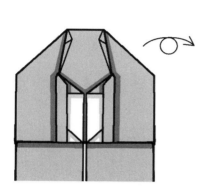

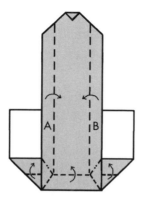

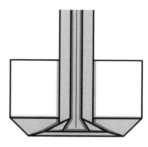

18 Turn over.

19 Valley fold sides A and B toward center and pull up the lower section.

20 Intermediate step.

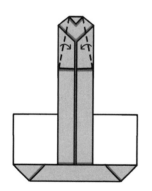

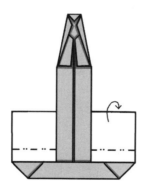

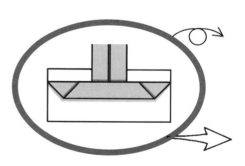

21 Valley fold the two sections inward as indicated.

22 Hill fold flap backward.

23 Turn over and see enlarged diagram of lower section.

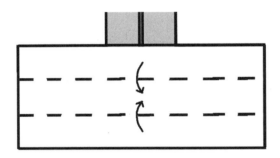

24 Valley fold the top and bottom sides inward.

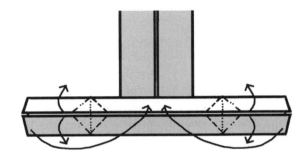

25 Open flaps up and fold inward toward the center.

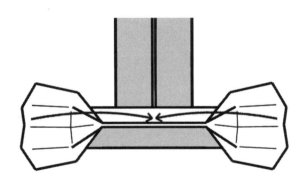

26 Intermediate step.

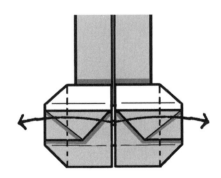

27 Valley fold both flaps outward.

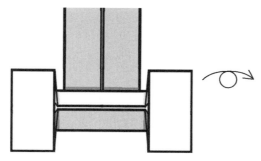

28 Turn over.

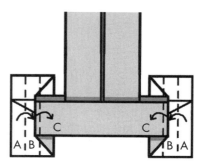

29 Valley fold areas A to B and then to C, on both sides.

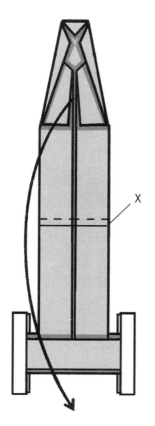

30 Valley fold the top section downward to a position slightly above point X (Diagram 1).

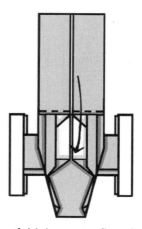

31 Valley fold the entire flap down.

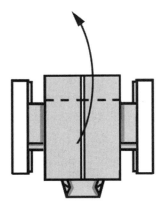

32 Lift flap back upward.

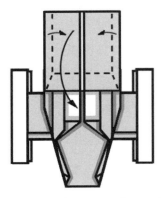

33 Narrow the two sides and fold forward simultaneously.

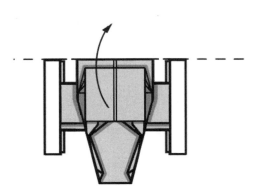

34 Pull back the entire section to reveal the pocket underneath.

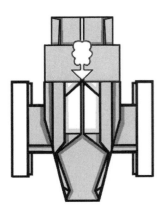

35 Inflate the pocket. (See picture of finished model.)

*Fold the small triangle section
downward to trap the door shut.*

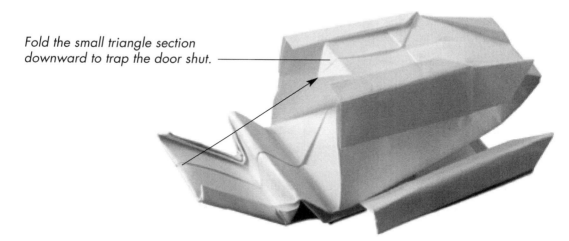

Finished model with shuttle door open.

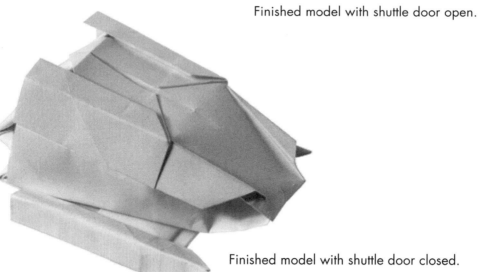

Finished model with shuttle door closed.

Shuttlecraft Type-6

Shuttlecraft Type-9

As seen in *Star Trek: Voyager.*

Begin with a water bomb base.

Water Bomb Base

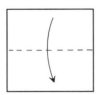

1a Begin with a square piece of paper. Valley fold paper in half.

2a Pull across the upper layer from the halfway line and squash open pocket.

TIP: Precrease valley fold and hill fold before folding across.

3a Turn over and repeat on the other side.

TIP: As in Step 2, precrease the paper prior to the actual fold.

4a Squash flat to complete a water bomb base.

5a Completed water bomb base.

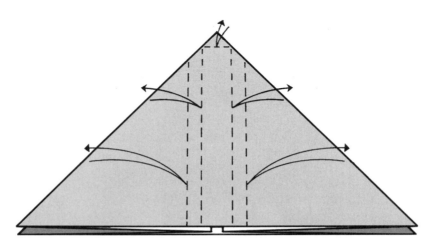

1 Precrease as indicated.

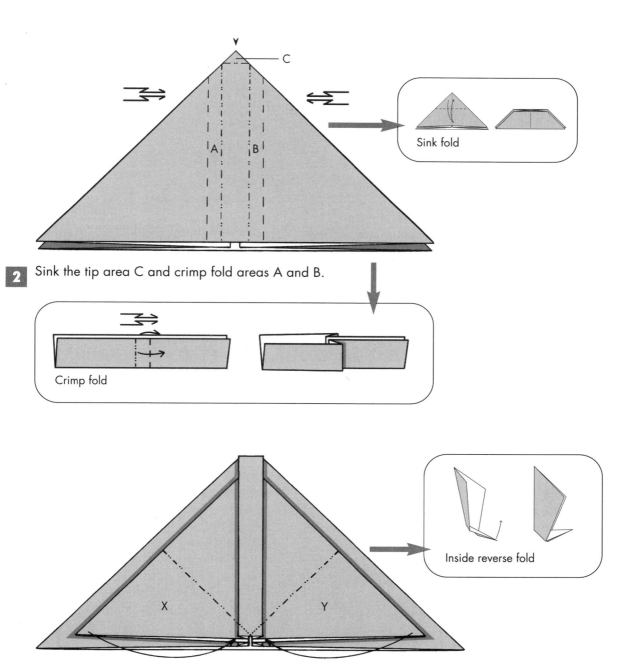

Sink fold

2 Sink the tip area C and crimp fold areas A and B.

Crimp fold

Inside reverse fold

3 Inside reverse fold areas X and Y completely inward.

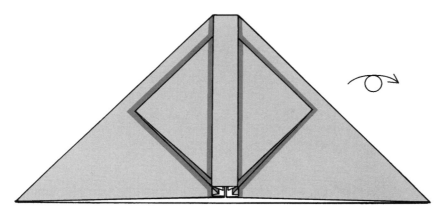

4 Turn over.

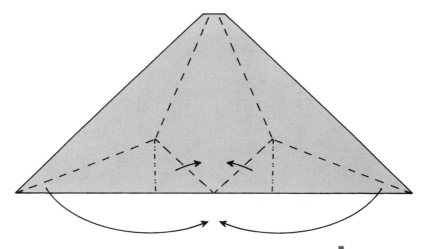

5 Rabbit's ear fold as indicated
(similar to Steps 10 through 15 of Starbase 1).

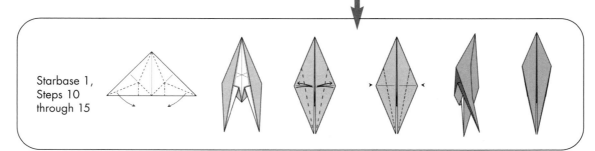

Starbase 1,
Steps 10
through 15

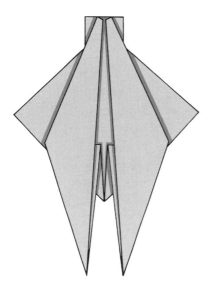

6 Intermediate step.

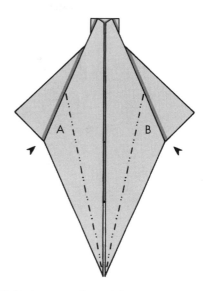

7 Sink areas A and B.

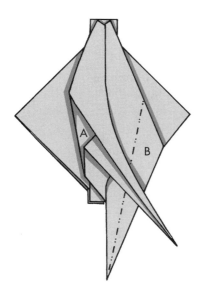

8 Completed sink on side A; repeat on side B.

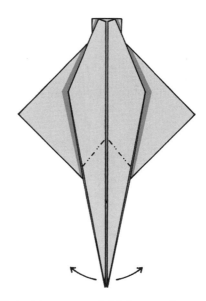

9 Inside reverse fold the two legs upward.

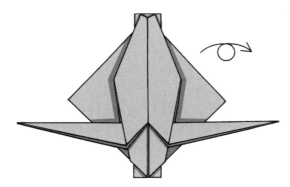

10 Turn over.

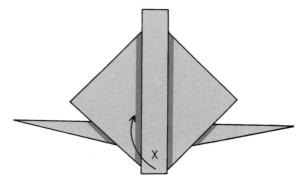

11 Slowly pull up flap X to reveal section Y underneath.

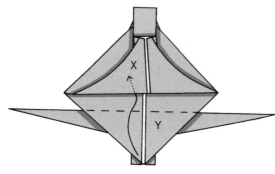

12 Valley fold Y upward to slip underneath flap X.

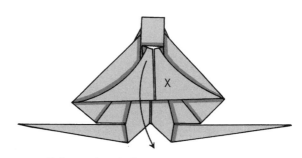

13 Pull flap X back down.

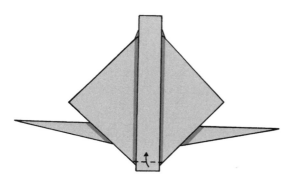

14 Valley fold the small bottom area up.

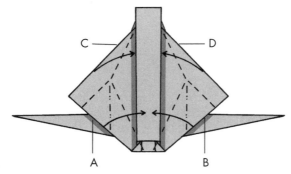

15 Valley fold edges A and B toward center while pulling edges C and D across simultaneously.

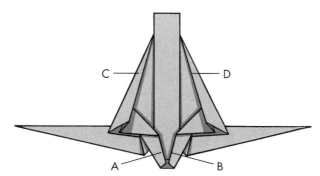

16 Intermediate step.

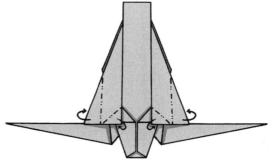

17 Hill fold the side sections back into the pockets located underneath, and hill fold the two small corners behind.

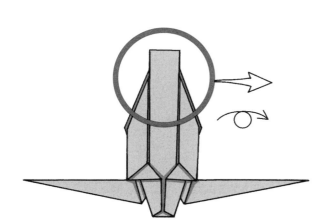

18 Turn over to fold the head section.

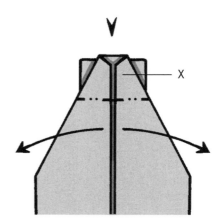

19 Open up flaps and inside reverse fold section X completely inward.

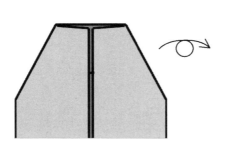

20 Turn back over.

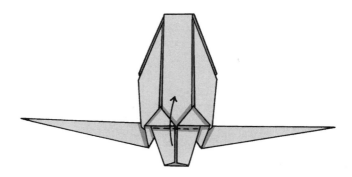

21 Valley fold bottom flap up.

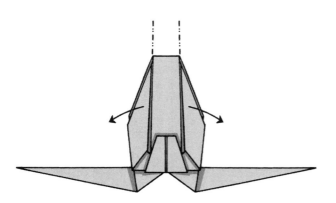

22 Hill fold the sides downward to form the two curved sides of the shuttlecraft.

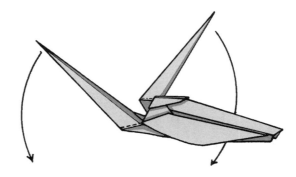

23 Side profile.
Valley fold both wings downward.

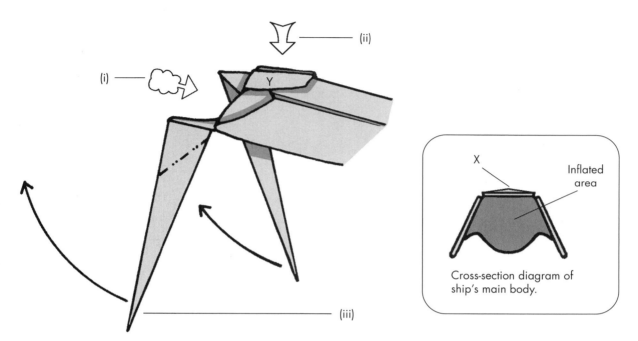

(i) ———
(ii)
Y
(iii)

X
Inflated area

Cross-section diagram of ship's main body.

24 (i) Insert pencil or finger into pocket to inflate body.
(ii) Push section Y downward to form a small valley shaped area.
(iii) Inside reverse fold legs backward.

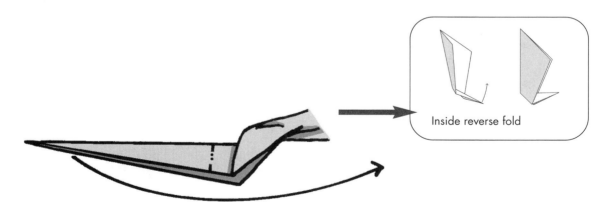

Inside reverse fold

25 Inside reverse fold legs back forward.

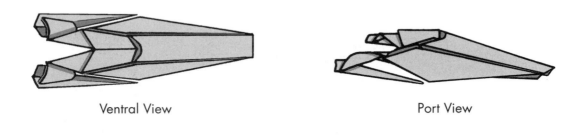

Ventral View   Port View

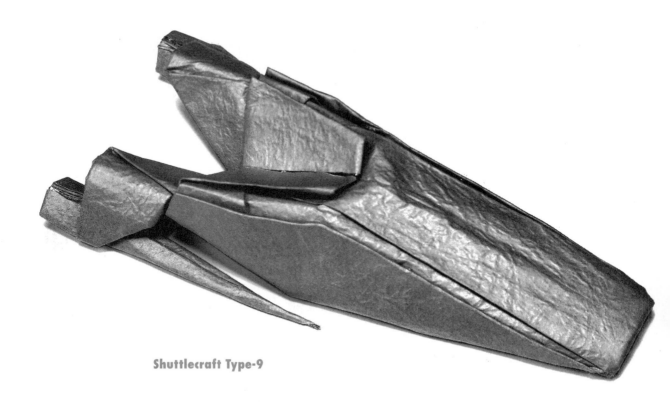

Shuttlecraft Type-9

ALLIED VESSELS
AND STATION

Deep Space 9

A three-piece model.

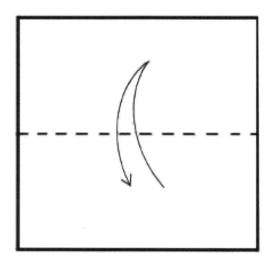

1 Begin with a square piece of paper. Precrease paper in half.

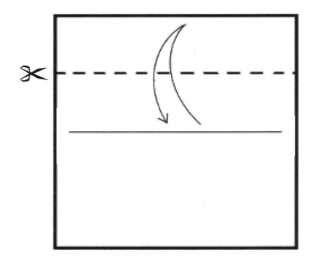

2 Precrease paper at quarter mark and cut paper at the dotted line.

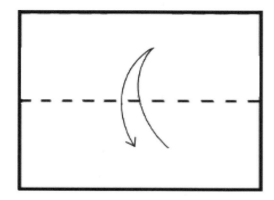

3 Precrease the cut paper in half.

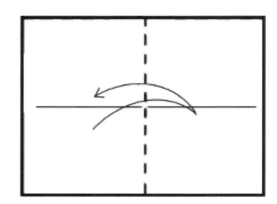

4 Precrease halfway across the paper.

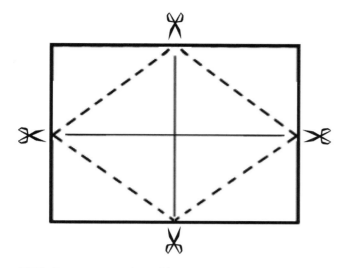

5 Cut paper at dotted lines.

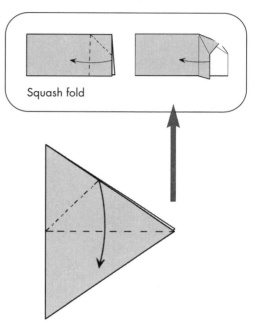

Squash fold

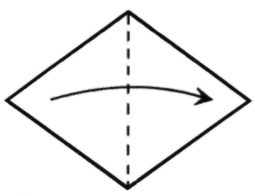

6 Fold across.

7 Lift top layer to squash open pocket.

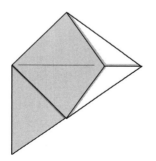

8 Turn over.

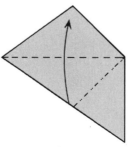

9 Repeat Steps 7 and 8.

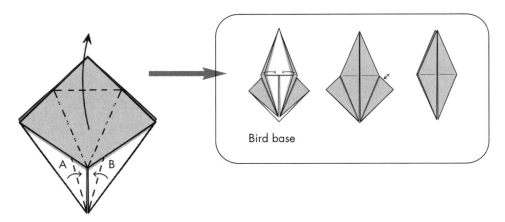

Bird base

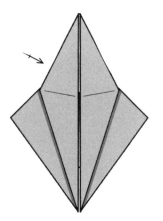

10 Lift top flap up—pulling in areas A and B (similar to a bird base fold).

11 Turn over, and repeat step on the other side.

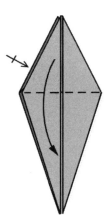

12 Valley fold upper flap down on both sides.

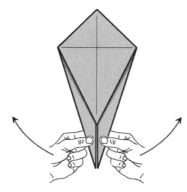

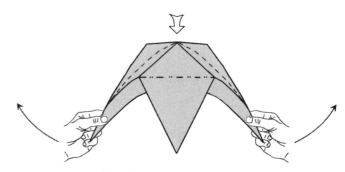

13 Pull both legs apart, open up, and collapse the center part slowly.

14 Push and sink in the center section.

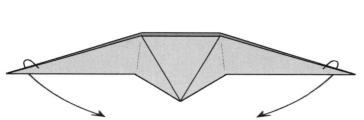

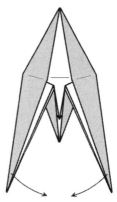

15 Close both arms back toward the center.

16 Intermediate step.

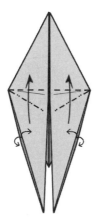

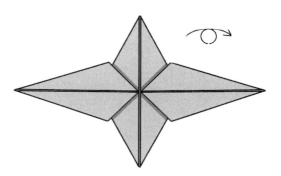

17 Lift and squash open both legs upward.
TIP: Precrease as shown before you lift and squash.

18 Turn over.

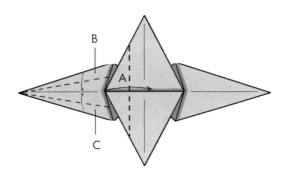

19 Valley fold area A across to just beyond the centerline, pulling in areas B and C simultaneously.

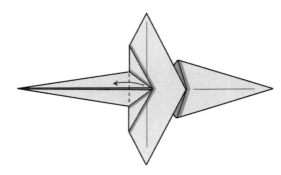

20 Fold flap back.

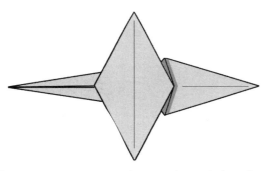

21 Repeat Steps 18 and 19 on the right-hand side.

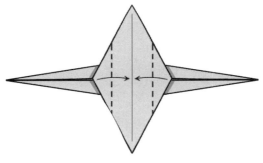

22 Valley fold both sections to the centerline.

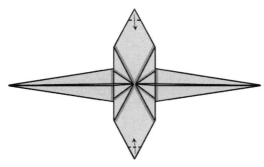

23 Valley fold the small top and bottom corners inward.

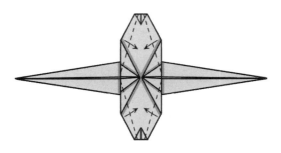

24 Valley fold all four sides inward.

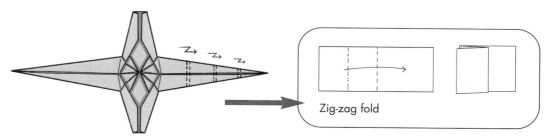

25 Zigzag fold in three different sections on the right arm.

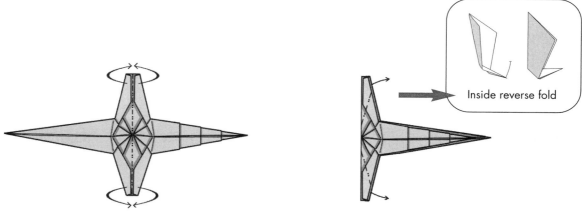

26 Fold the two halves together.

27 Inward reverse fold the top and bottom sections.

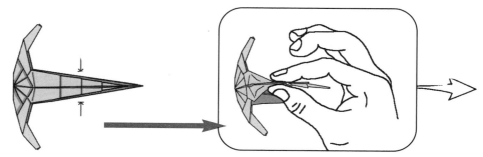

28 Squeeze the two halves of the arm together.

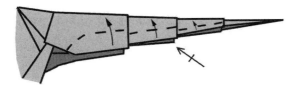

29 Valley fold each of the three sections upward, and repeat the same on the other side.

30 Pull and bend arm slowly into a circular curve.

31 Completed arm.

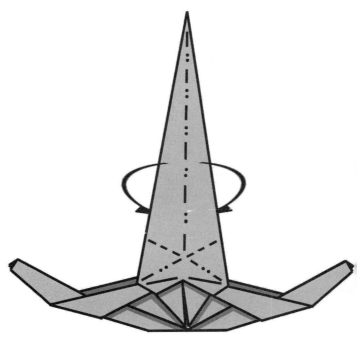

32 Hill fold the two halves of the other arm together as indicated.

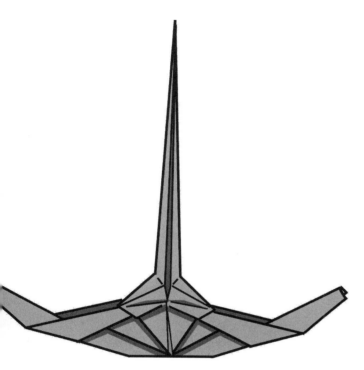

33 Rotate the arm to a top-down view.

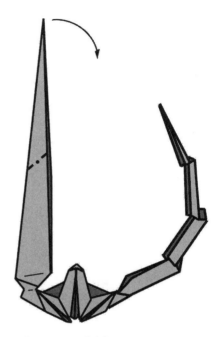

34 Inside reverse fold arm across.

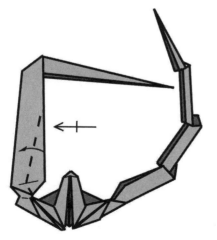

35 Fold the top small section across, and repeat on the other side.

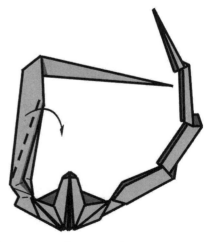

36 Rotate arm downward.

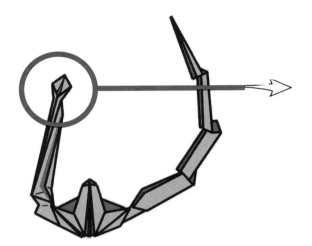

37 Follow Steps 37 through 42 to fold center section.

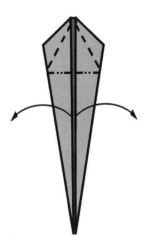

38 Open up flaps and fold upward.

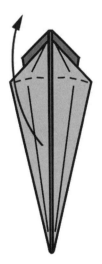

39 Intermediate step—continue to fold flap upward.

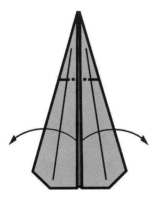

40 Open up flaps and fold the tip section down.

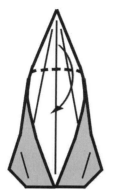

41 Intermediate step.

42 Close flaps back.

43 Finished section.

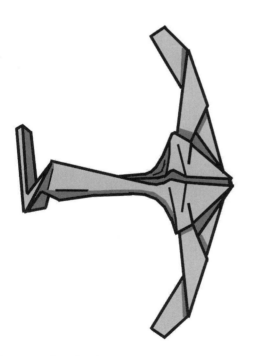

Repeat Steps 1 through 44 twice to fold two additional identical sections.

44 Completed side profile of the entire section.

The joining diagrams for the three sections. First join sections A and B.

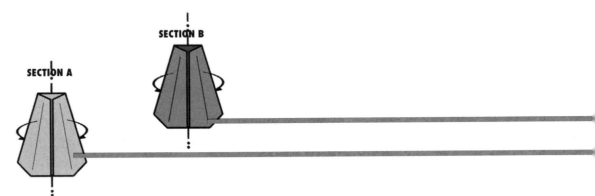

45 Slightly (hill) bend both sections at the centerline.

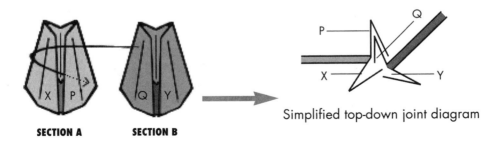

Simplified top-down joint diagram

46 Insert section Q into pocket P. (X and Y are reference points only)
TIP: This would be a good place for a dot of glue.

47 Joined middle section of A and B.

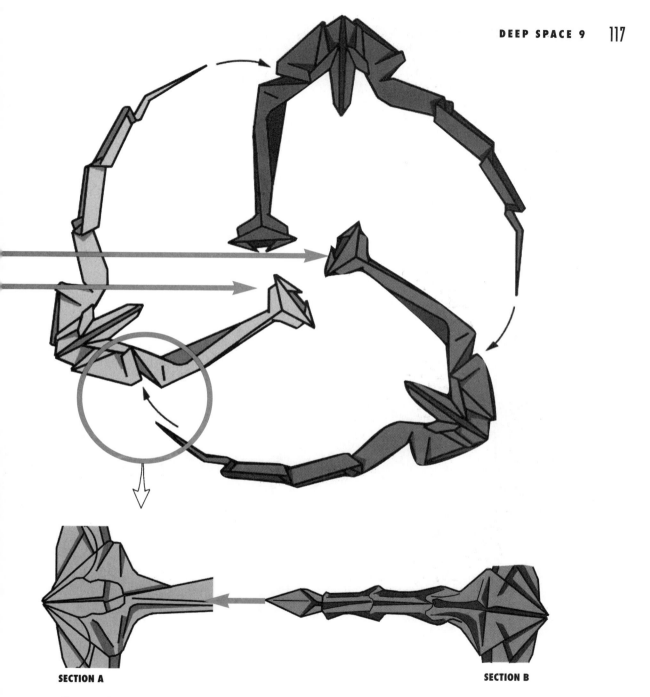

SECTION A

SECTION B

48 Pull open the side section of A to reveal the inside gap/pocket, and insert B's arm into the gap/pocket.

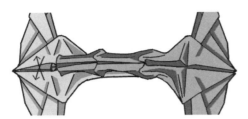

49 Close the side section back, after inserting section B.

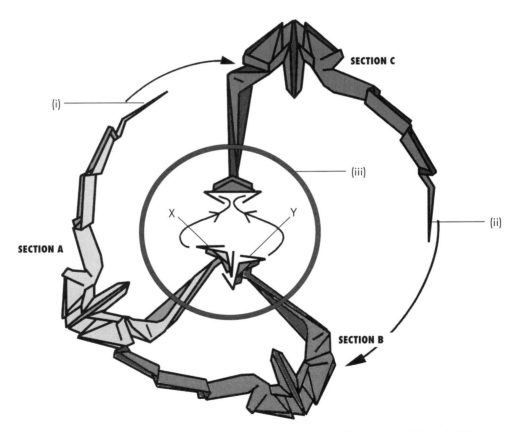

50 (i) Insert section A's arm into the side pocket at section C (Diagrams 47 and 48).
(ii) Insert section C's arm into the side pocket at section B (Diagrams 47 and 48).
(iii) Insert sections X and Y (Diagram 46) into the front pocket at section C.

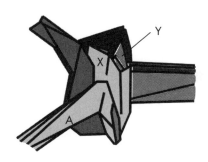

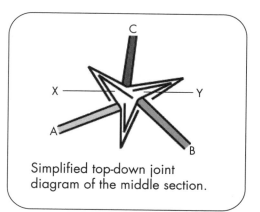

Simplified top-down joint diagram of the middle section.

51 Completed middle section.

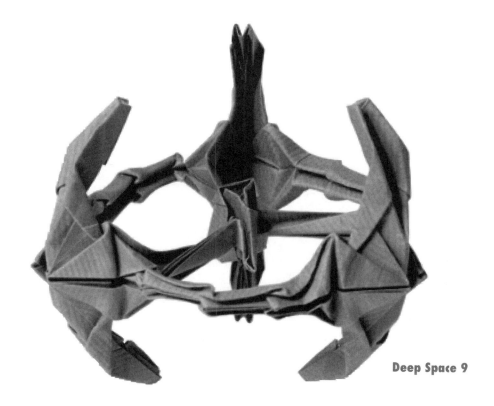

Deep Space 9

Klingon Battle Cruiser

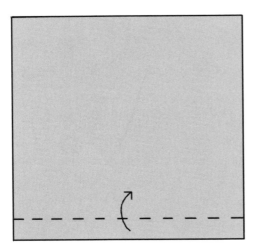

1 Begin with a square piece of paper; valley fold lower section up to approximately $1/12$ the width of the paper.

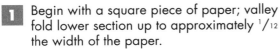

2 Precrease the two bottom corners.

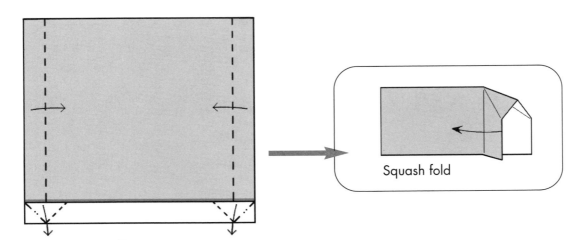

Squash fold

3 Valley fold the side sections inward—the same width as the lower section—and squash open the two bottom corners.

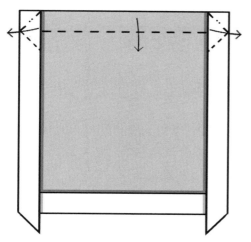

4 Repeat Steps 1 through 3 for the top flap.

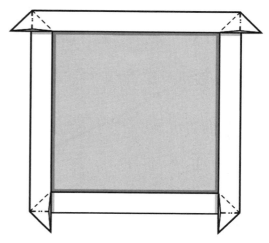

5 Squash open the corners into a small preliminary base.

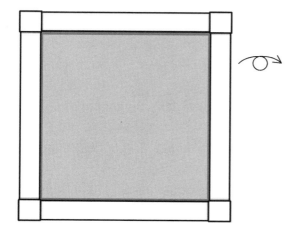

6 Turn over.

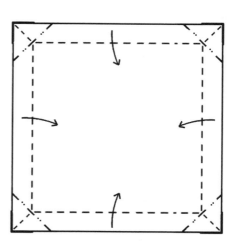

7 Valley fold all four sides inward the same width and repeat Steps 1 through 6.

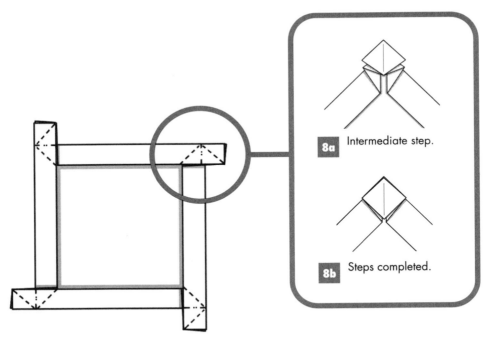

8a   Intermediate step.

8b   Steps completed.

8 Squash open pockets, forming another small preliminary base (diagrams 8a and 8b).

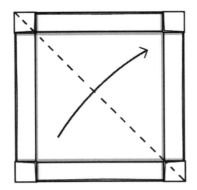

9 Valley fold the entire paper into a preliminary base.

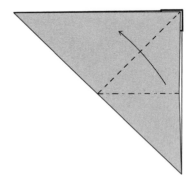

10 Intermediate step—pull top layer across and squash open pocket.

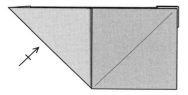

11 Repeat Step 10 on the other side to complete the base.

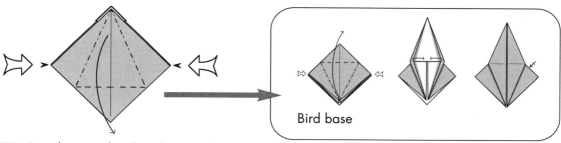

12 Turn the completed preliminary base into a bird base.

Bird base

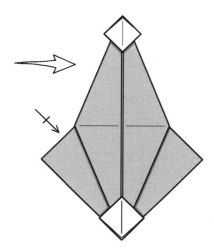

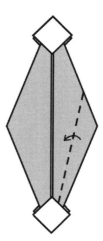

13 Repeat step on the other side to complete the bird base.

TIP: The two wings/flaps (the pieces that can be separated) should be at the bottom.

14 Valley fold the right-side edge toward the centerline.

TIP: Fold the flaps underneath the small bases at the bottom.

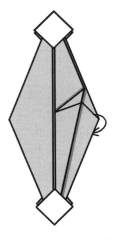

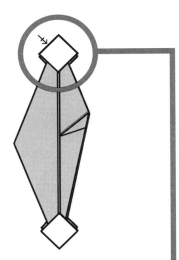

15 Repeat on the other side.

16 Follow steps 16a to 16e for the two top flaps.

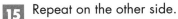

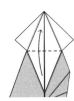

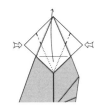

16a Pull down top layer and squash in the sides for a small bird base fold.

TIP: Precrease the hill and valley folds, as shown.

16b Fold flap upward.

16c Pull the second layer upward to form a second small bird base.

TIP: Lifting the upper layer up is the only way to create the second small bird base.

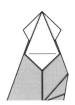

16d Fold top flap down.

16e Steps completed. Repeat steps 16a through 16d on the flap behind.

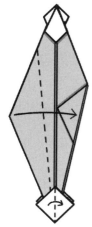

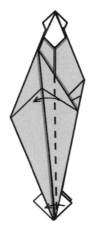

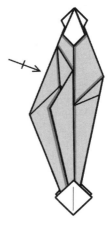

17 Valley fold left-side edge all the way across to the right-side edge.

18 Fold flap back across from the centerline position.

19 Repeat Steps 17 and 18 on the flap behind.

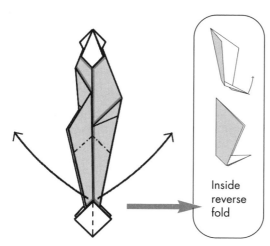

Inside reverse fold

20 Inside reverse folds both legs upward.

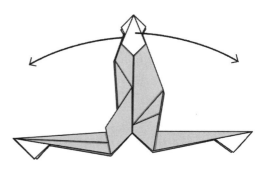

21 Pull the two top flaps apart slowly.

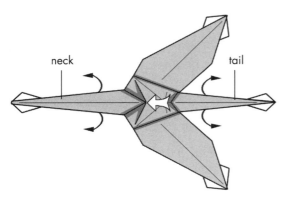

neck

tail

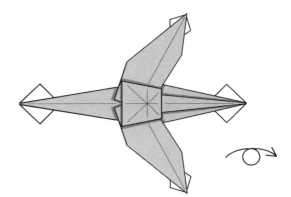

22 Top-down view—open up and press flat both the neck and tail flaps, and then press, where shown, the main body section gently to flatten the entire model.

23 Turn over.

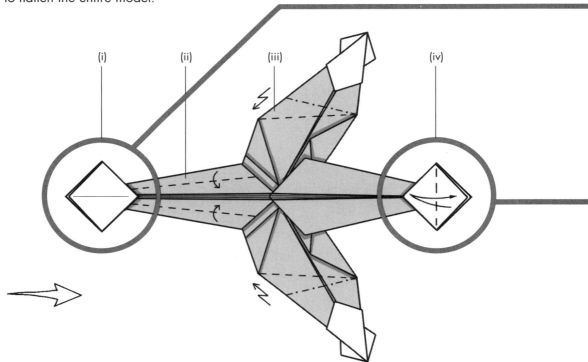

(i) (ii) (iii) (iv)

24
(i) Follow Steps 16a through 16e for the forward section.
(ii) Narrow the upper part by valley folding the two side edges toward the centerline position.
(iii) Zigzag fold the two wing sections as indicated.
(iv) Precrease the small base as shown and follow diagrams 24a through 24c carefully to fold the aft section.

16a Pull down top layer and squash in the sides for a small bird base fold.

TIP: Precrease the hill and valley folds, as shown.

16b Fold flap upward.

16c Pull the second layer upward to form a second small bird base.

TIP: Lifting the upper layer upward is the only way to create the second small bird base.

16d Fold top flap down.

16e Steps completed.

24a Pull the top layer down slowly to flatten out the entire section.

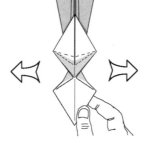

24b Pull out slowly . . . pushing out the two sides.

24c Completed section.

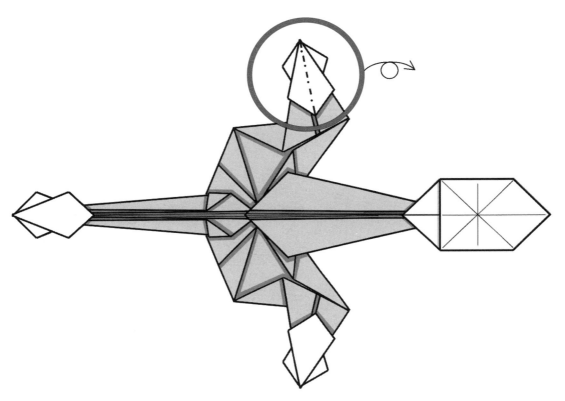

25 Turn over and follow carefully Diagrams 26 through 30 for the wing/nacelle section.

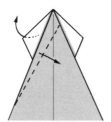

26 Flip over the back section toward the front.

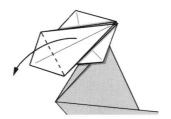

27 Valley fold flap forward.

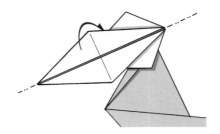

28 Hill fold flap in half.

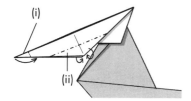

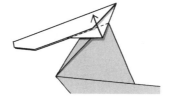
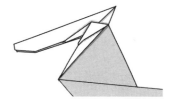

29 (i) Hill fold the tip end inward.
(ii) Hill fold the two lower sections inward.

30 Valley fold flap upward, and repeat on the other side.

31 Completed wing/nacelle section.

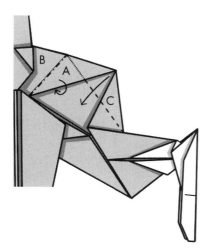
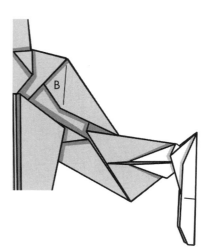

32 Hill fold flap A into the pocket located underneath layer B, while pulling down section C simultaneously.

33 Completed wing section. Repeat Steps 26 through 30 on the other wing.

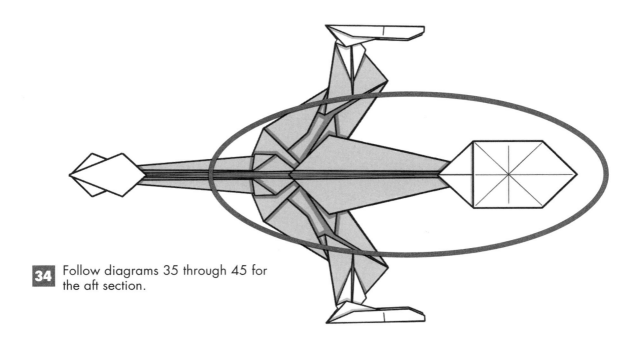

34 Follow diagrams 35 through 45 for the aft section.

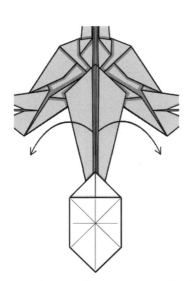

35 Open up the two flaps out completely.

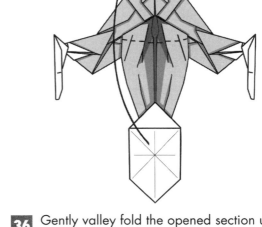

36 Gently valley fold the opened section upward.

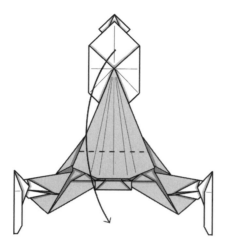

37 Valley fold flap back downward.

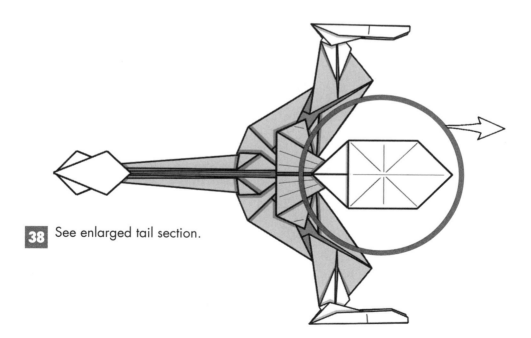

38 See enlarged tail section.

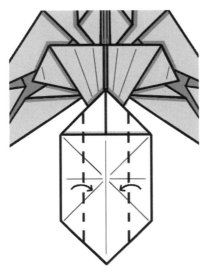

39 Valley fold the two sides toward center.

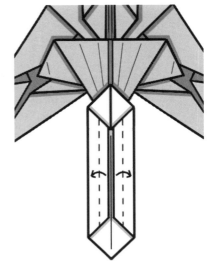

40 Valley fold flap back outward.

41 Insert flap A underneath flap B.

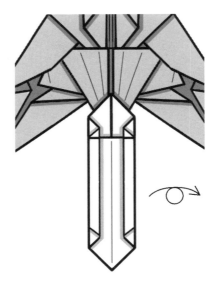

42 Turn over.

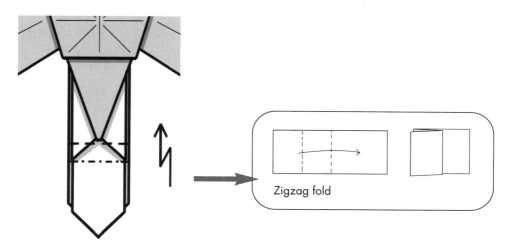

Zigzag fold

43 Zigzag fold as indicated.

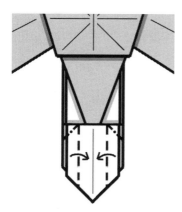

44 Valley fold the two sides toward the center while squashing flat the two small top corners simultaneously.

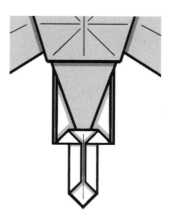

45 Completed section.

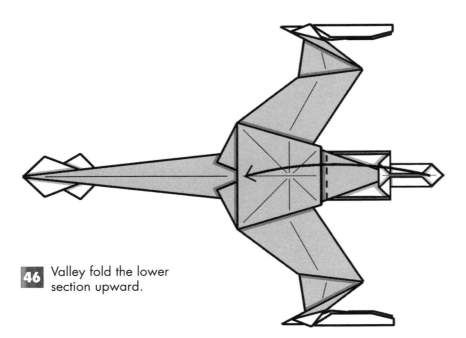

46 Valley fold the lower section upward.

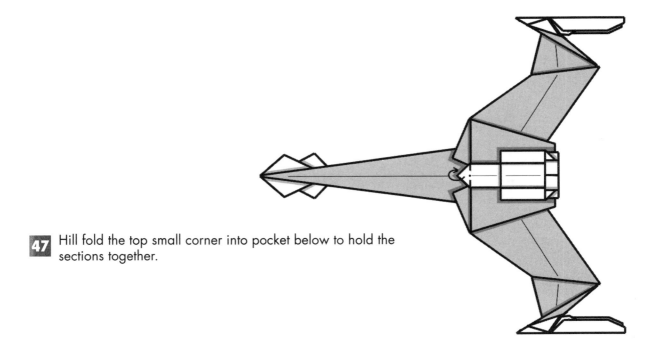

47 Hill fold the top small corner into pocket below to hold the sections together.

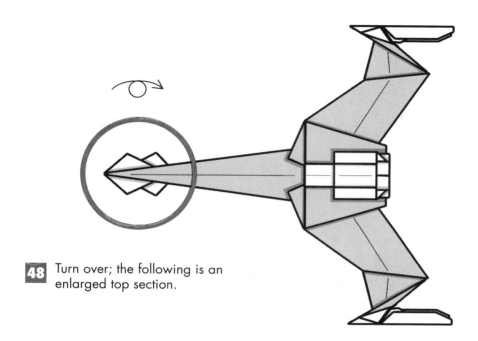

48 Turn over; the following is an enlarged top section.

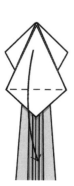

49 Valley fold the top flap downward.

50 Valley fold the entire section upward.

51 Valley fold the two small side corners.

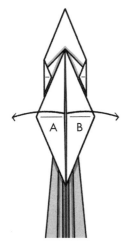

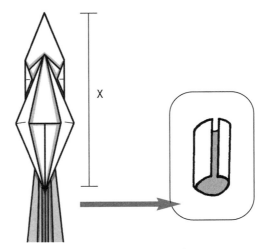

52 Open up flaps A and B slowly.

53 Roll down section X into the opened area.

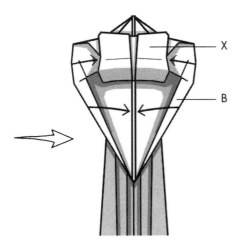

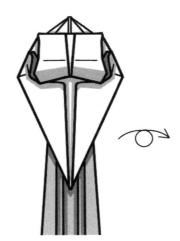

54 Close back flaps A and B.

55 Turn over.

56 Valley fold the small top corner section.

57 Completed forward section of the ship.

58 Bottom/side view.

Klingon Battle Cruiser

Klingon Bird-of-Prey

Begin with a bird base.

Bird Base

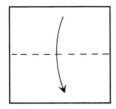

1a Begin with a square piece of paper. Valley fold paper in half.

2a Valley fold right corner down to the bottom edge.

3a Hill fold the other corner down to the bottom edge on the opposite side.

4a Open up the center pocket by pushing in from both sides.

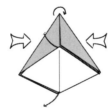

5a Intermediate step—continue to open up, rotate paper around, and squash model flat.

6a Completed preliminary base.

7a Precrease lines as indicated.

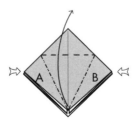

8a Lift up front flap and push in areas A and B toward center.

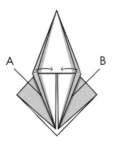

9a Intermediate step, continue to push in areas A and B toward center.

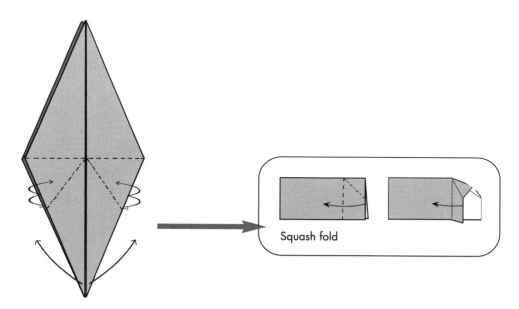

1 Squash open pockets on both arms and fold upward.

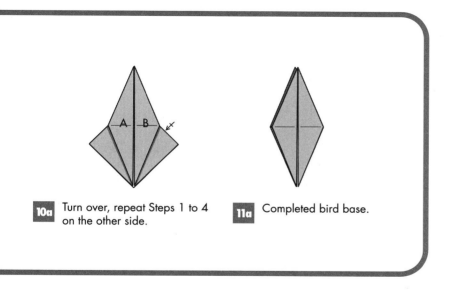

10a Turn over, repeat Steps 1 to 4 on the other side.

11a Completed bird base.

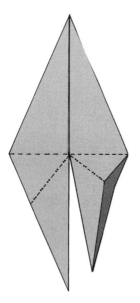

2 Intermediate step.

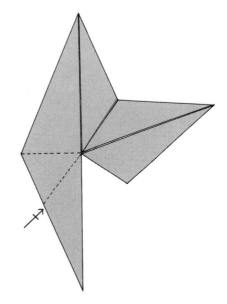

3 Repeat on the other arm.

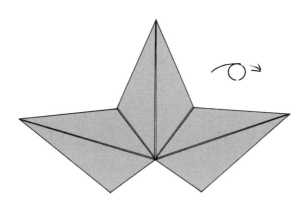

4 Turn over.

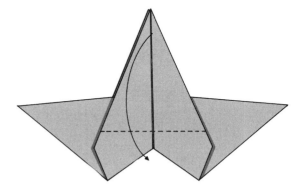

5 Valley fold front flap down.

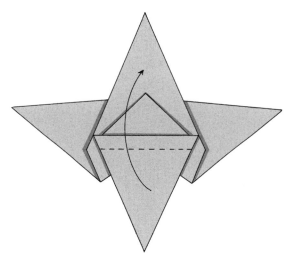

6 Valley fold flap back up.

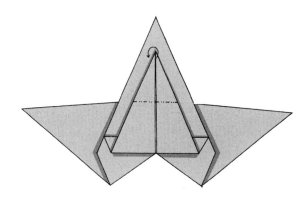

7 Hill fold flap behind.

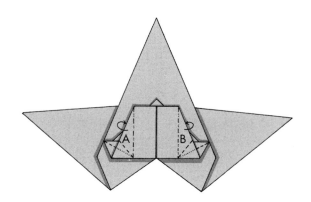

8 Hill fold areas A and B behind to form a central rectangular area.

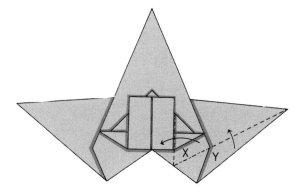

9 Fold flap X across and pull up area Y simultaneously.

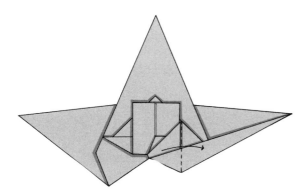

10 Fold flap back across.

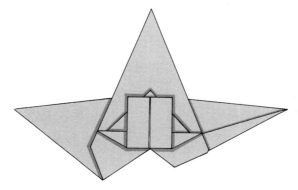

11 Repeat Steps 9 through 10 on the left-hand side.

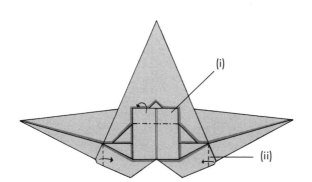

12 (i) Hill fold flap behind as indicated.
(ii Valley fold the two bottom corners inward.

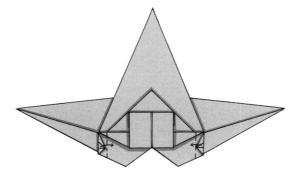

13 Valley fold bottom corners inward again.

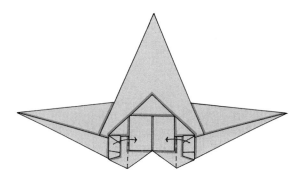

14 Valley fold bottom corners farther inward.

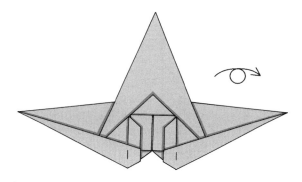

15 Turn over.

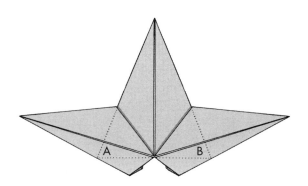

16 Follow the next four steps carefully to pull the inside flaps A and B out onto the front.

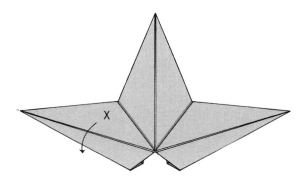

17 Valley fold X down.

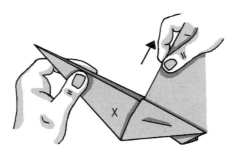

18 Slowly pull inside flap A (Diagram 17) out.

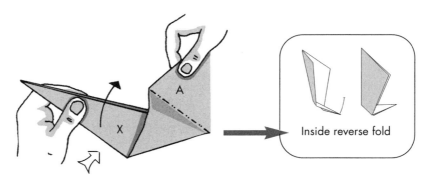

Inside reverse fold

19 Inside reverse fold flap X back up.

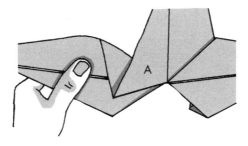

20 Intermediate step.

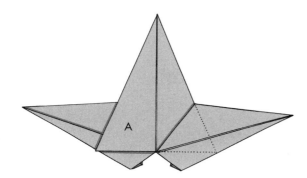

21 Repeat Steps 16 through 20 on right-hand side.

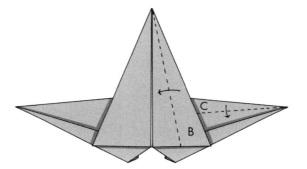

22 Valley fold area B across and pull down area C simultaneously.

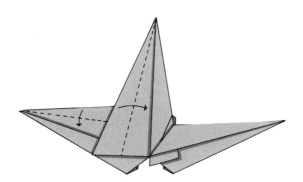

23 Repeat Step 22 on the left-hand side.

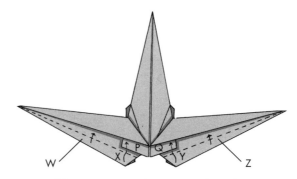

24 Fold areas W and Z upward, with corners X and Y to fold underneath flaps P and Q.

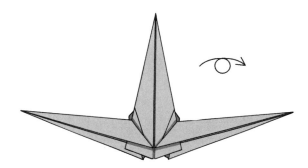

25 Turn over.

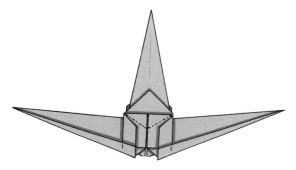

26 Push in the center area to form a small hill/mountain shaped area.

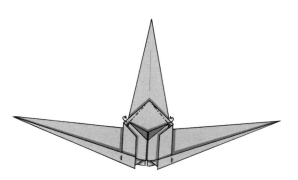

27 Hill fold both sides behind to lock in the small hill section.

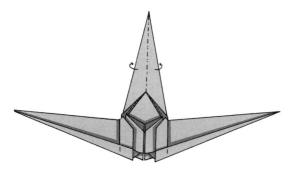

28 Hill fold the two sides together. (See Diagram 29 for a side profile.)

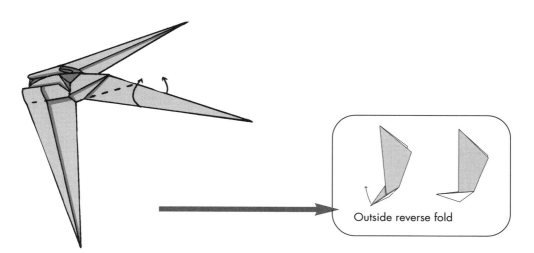

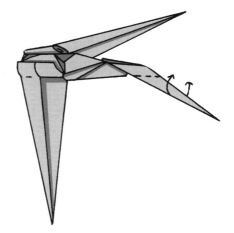

Outside reverse fold

29 Side profile.
Outside reverse fold upward.

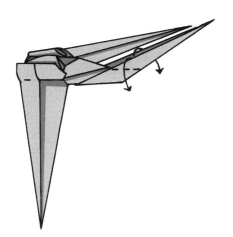

30 Outside reverse fold downward.

31 Outside reverse fold upward.

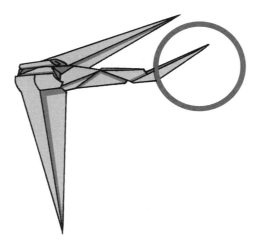

32 Following is an enlarged forward section.

33 Outside reverse fold to open flat front section.

34 Open up bottom flaps.

35 Following is an enlarged command section.

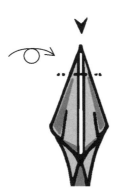

36 Sink tip section.

37 Finished head section of the ship.

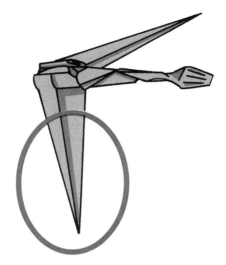

38 Following is an enlarged wing section.

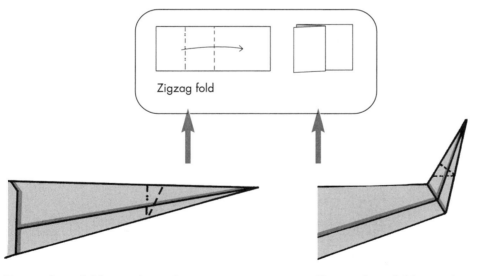

Zigzag fold

39 Zigzag/step fold as indicated.

40 Zigzag/step fold as indicated.

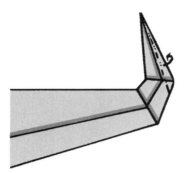

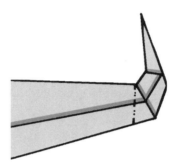

41 Hill fold flap behind to narrow down the wing cannon section.

42 Fold to a right angle (90 degrees) to finish the cannon section.

Repeat Steps 39 through 42 on the other wing.

Klingon Bird-of-Prey

SHIPS OF THE GALAXY

The Borg Cube

This is a classic fold well known to schoolchildren all over the world. It is also known as the balloon or water bomb, from which the base, water bomb, gets its name.

Begin with a water bomb base.

Water Bomb Base

1a Begin with a square piece of paper. Valley fold paper in half.

2a Pull across the upper layer from the halfway line and squash open pocket.

TIP: Precrease valley fold and hill fold before folding across.

3a Turn over and repeat on the other side.

TIP: As in Step 2, precrease the paper prior to the actual fold.

4a Squash flat to complete a water bomb base.

5a Completed water bomb base.

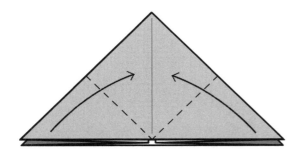

1 Lift and valley fold the bottom edges up toward the centerline.

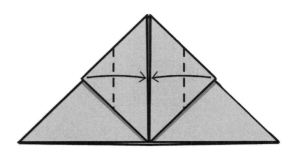

2 Valley fold the two side corners toward the centerline.

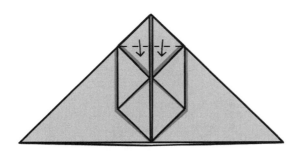

3 Valley fold the two triangular flaps down.

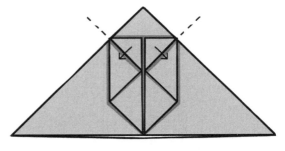

4 Valley fold the two triangles down.

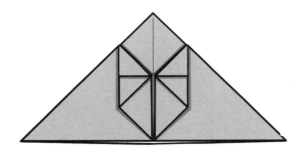

5 Tuck the two triangles into the pockets located underneath.

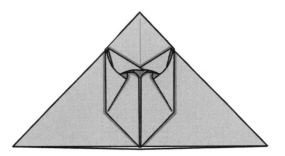

6 Intermediate step—continue to tuck triangles into the pockets.

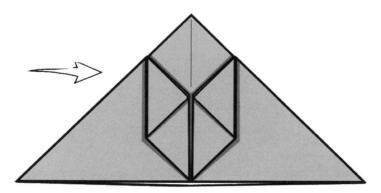

7 Turn over and repeat Steps 1 through 6 on the other side.

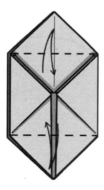

8 Precrease firmly the top and bottom corners toward the center point.

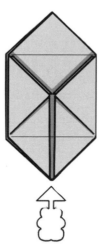

9 Inflate the cube by blowing air into the small hole located at the bottom.

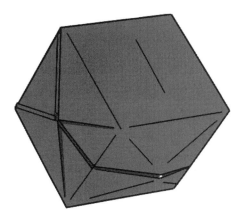

10 Pinch the edges to form a cube shape.

The Borg Cube

Ferengi Marauder

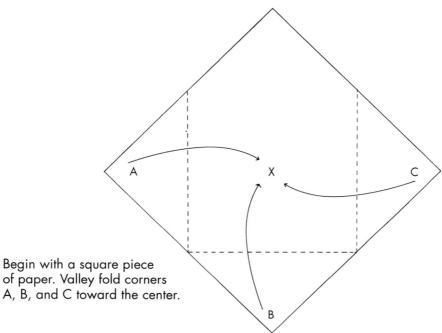

1 Begin with a square piece of paper. Valley fold corners A, B, and C toward the center.

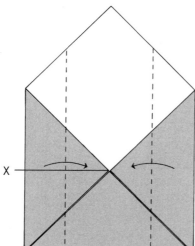

2 Valley fold sides toward the centerline.

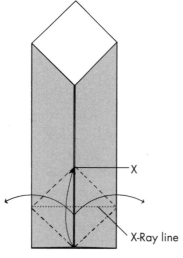

3 Open up flaps and fold bottom edge up toward midpoint X position.

TIP: Precrease hill and valley folds, as shown.

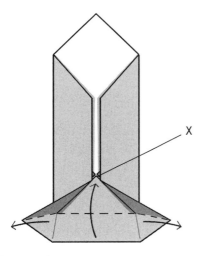

4 Intermediate step.

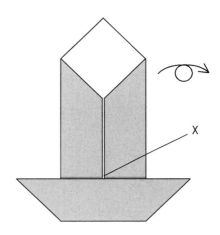

5 Turn over.

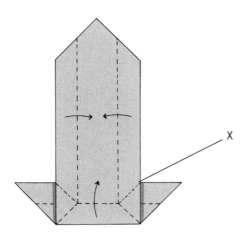

6 Valley fold sides toward the center and pull the lower edge up toward the point X position.

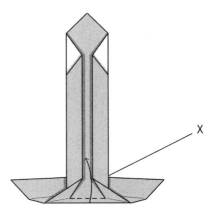

7 Intermediate step—continue to fold lower edge upward toward X while closing the two sides toward the center.

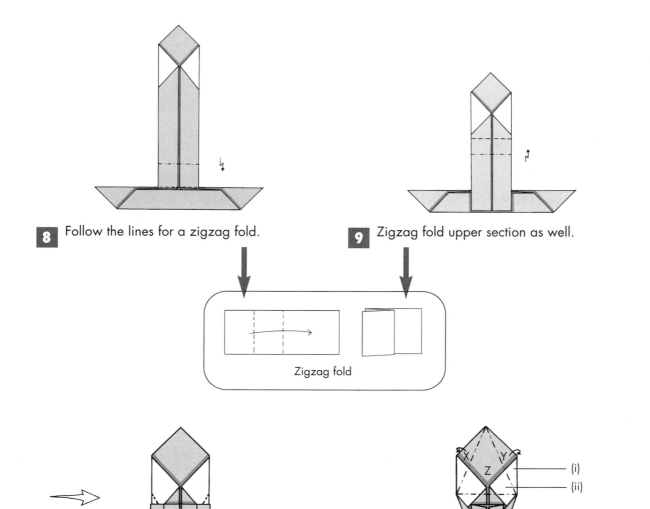

8 Follow the lines for a zigzag fold.

9 Zigzag fold upper section as well.

Zigzag fold

10 Fold sides toward center, squashing open the upper and lower corners simultaneously.

11
(i) Hill fold areas X and Y behind to form a triangular area.
(ii) Hill fold the resulting triangle Z behind.
(iii) Insert the lower section into the pocket located underneath.

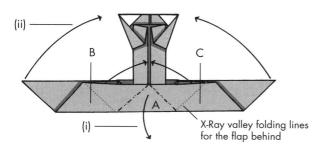

(ii)

B   C

A

(i)

X-Ray valley folding lines
for the flap behind

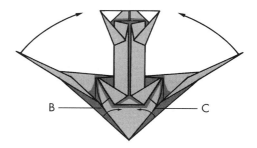

B   C

12 (i) Pull down flap A to open pocket, so
that edges B and C meet at the
centerline position.
(ii) Lift up the two sides simultaneously.

13 Intermediate step—continue to close edges
B and C toward the center.

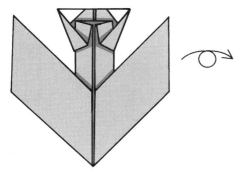

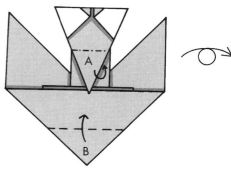

A

B

14 Turn over.

15 (i) Hill fold section A into the pocket located
underneath.
(ii) Valley fold section B upward and turn over.

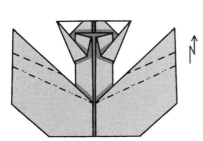

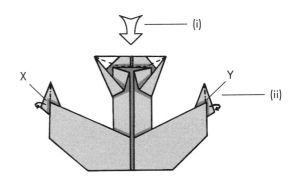

16 Follow the lines for a zigzag fold on both corners.

17 (i) Push in top section to form a 3-D curved section.
(ii) Hill fold sections X and Y behind to form the wing cannons.

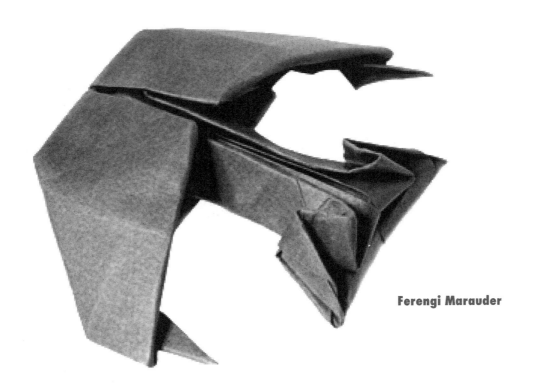

Ferengi Marauder

Cardassian
Galor-class Warship

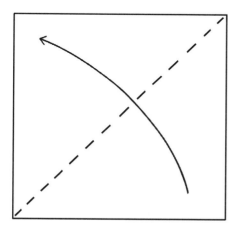

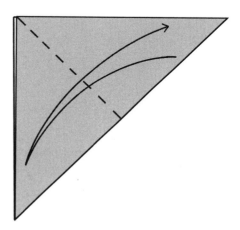

1 Begin with a square piece of paper. Fold paper in half across the diagonal line.

2 Precrease paper in half.

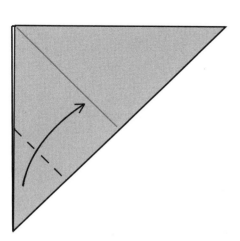

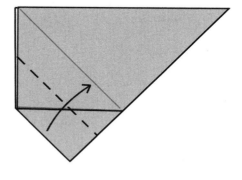

3 Fold the left corner to the centerline.

4 Fold the left edge to the centerline.

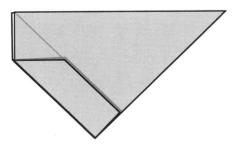

5 Open paper back out to the triangle.

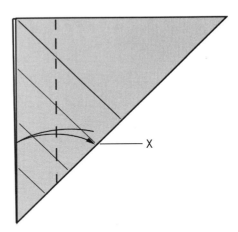

6 Precrease the left edge toward point X.

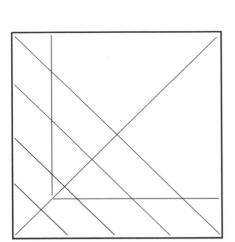

7 Open paper back out to a square.

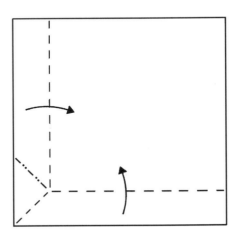

8 Use the precreased line and valley fold sides inward as indicated.

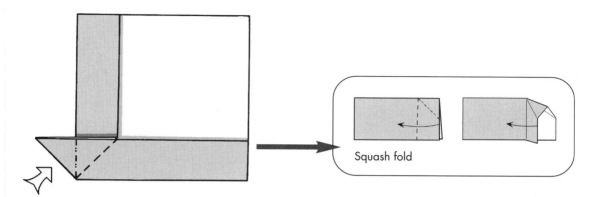

Squash fold

9 Squash open pocket to form a square.

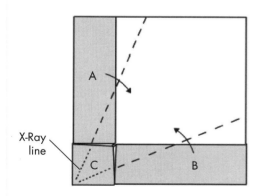

X-Ray
line

A

C

B

10 Valley fold areas A and B toward the diagonal line and places the flaps underneath section C.

TIP: The square C should not be folded.

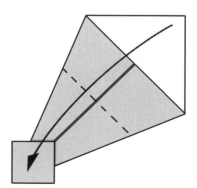

11 Valley fold in half.

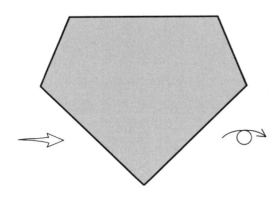

12 Turn over.

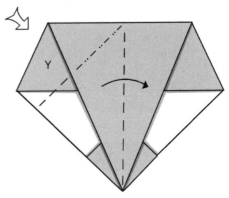

13 Fold the top layer across and squash open section Y simultaneously.

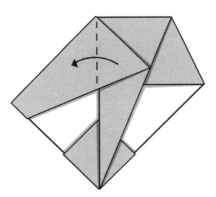

14 Fold flap back across.

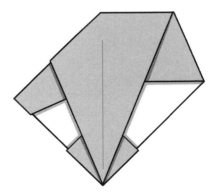

15 Repeat Steps 13 and 14 on the right-hand side.

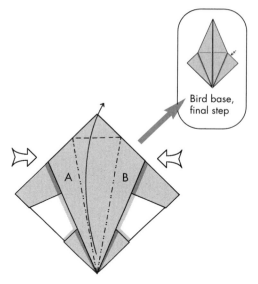

Bird base, final step

16 Pull front flap upward and squash in section A and B simultaneously.

TIP: This step is similar to the final step of a bird base.

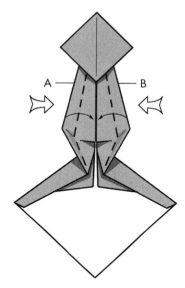

17 Intermediate step—Slowly pull the flap up while gently valley folding sections A and B inward.

TIP: Fold sections A and B underneath the top square section.

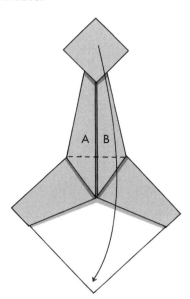

18 Valley fold top flap downward.

TIP: The paper will get slightly bulky.

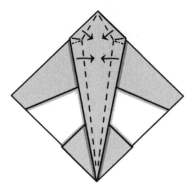

19 Narrow the middle section by valley folding both sides toward the center.

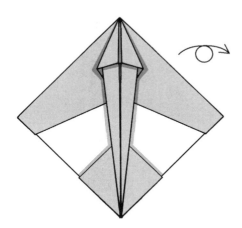

20 Turn over.

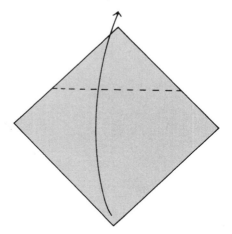

21 Valley fold flap up.

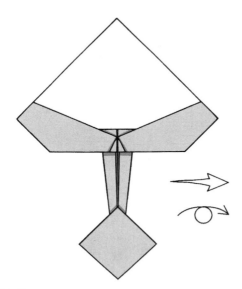

22 Turn over.

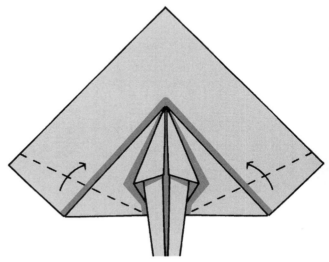

23 Enlarged upper section. Valley fold the two lower corners upward.

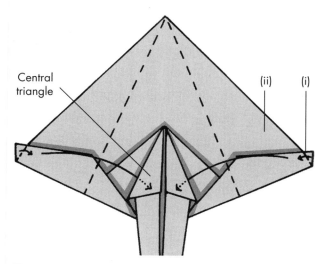

Central triangle

(ii) (i)

24 (i) Valley fold the two small corners inward.
(ii) Valley fold the two sides to the center and slip the flaps underneath the central triangular section.

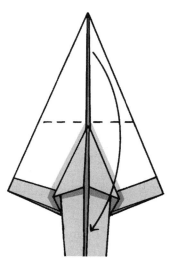

25 Valley fold flap downward.

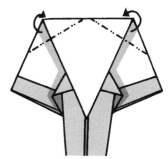

26 Hill fold the two corner sections behind.

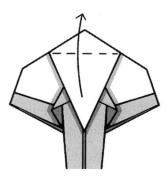

27 Valley fold flap upward.

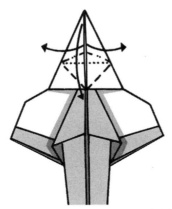

28 Open up flap and valley fold flap forward.
TIP: Gently precreasing the fold as shown makes the final fold crisper.

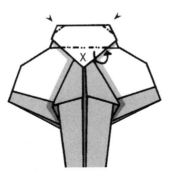

29 Sink in the two small corners, and hill fold flap X underneath.

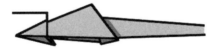

30 Side profile of forward section.

Aft Section

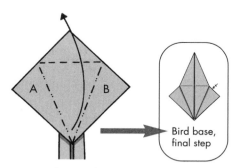

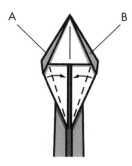

31 Pull flap up and squash in sides A and B.
TIP: This step is similar to the final step of a bird base.

Bird base, final step

32 Intermediate step—Slowly pulling up the flap while gently valley folding sections A and B inward.

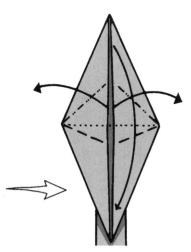

33 Open up flaps and valley fold flap downward.
TIP: Gently precreasing the folds as shown makes the final fold crisper.

34 Hill fold flap behind.

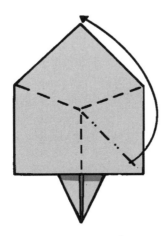

35 Follow the lines and pull flap upward.

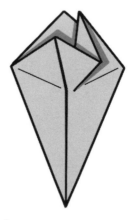

36 Intermediate step.

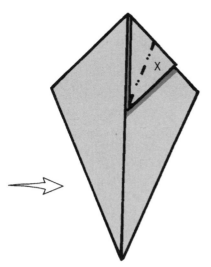

37 Squash open pocket X located at the front.

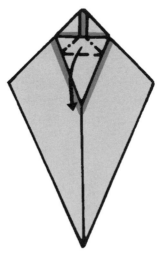

38 Pull down and squash open pocket.

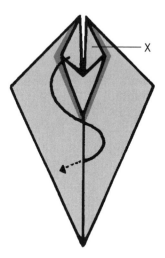

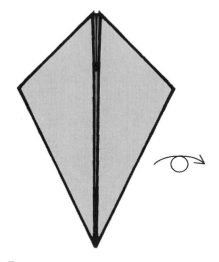

39 Slip the entire section X into the flaps located behind.

40 Turn over.

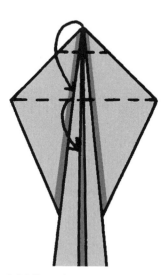

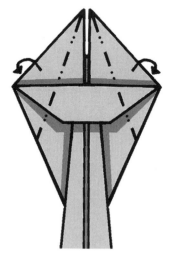

41 Valley fold flap down twice as indicated.

42 Hill fold sides behind.

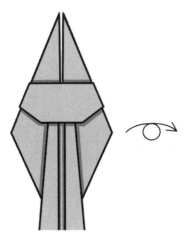

43 Turn over.

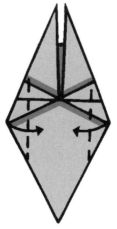

44 Valley fold sides toward the center.

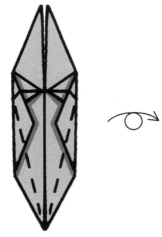

45 Valley fold sides inward and turn over.

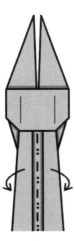

46 Hill fold the two sides together.
(See finished diagram.)

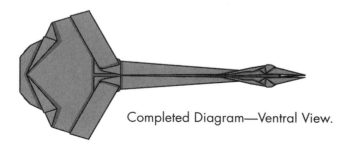

Completed Diagram—Ventral View.

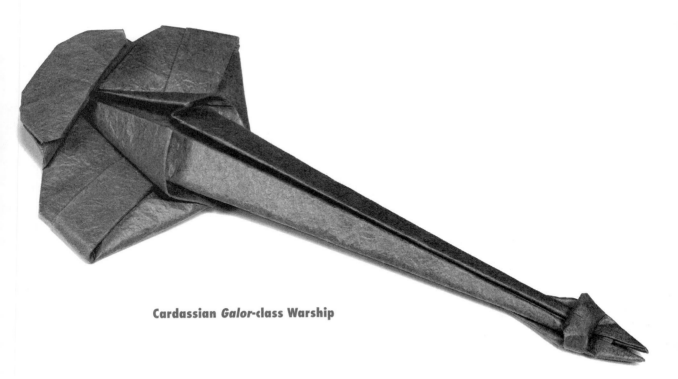

Cardassian *Galor*-class Warship

Jem'Hadar Attack Ship

Cut a square piece of paper in half to begin.

Water Bomb Base

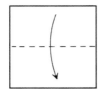

1a Begin with a square piece of paper. Valley fold paper in half.

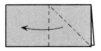

2a Pull across the upper layer from the halfway line and squash open pocket.

TIP: Precrease valley fold and hill fold before folding across.

3a Turn over and repeat on the other side.

TIP: As in Step 2, precrease the paper prior to the actual fold.

4a Squash flat to complete a water bomb base.

5a Completed water bomb base.

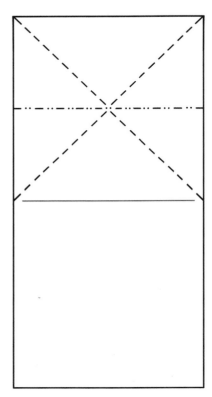

1 Fold the upper square into a water bomb base.

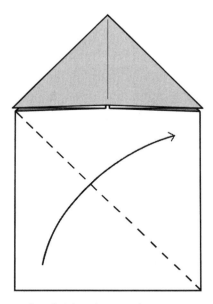

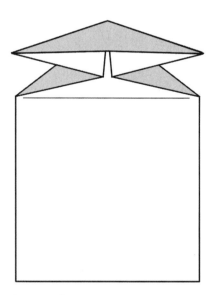

2 Intermediate step.

3 Valley fold a diagonal crease.

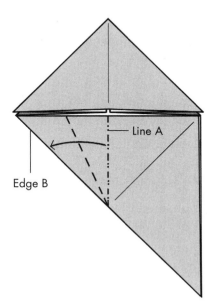

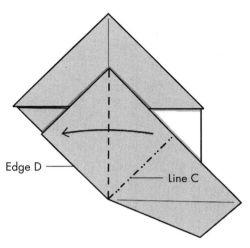

4 Fold line A across to meet edge B.

5 Similar to Step 4—fold line C across to meet edge D.

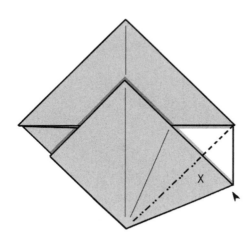

6 Reverse fold section X inward (similar to that of a sink fold).

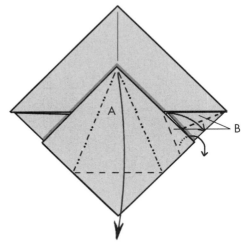

7 Pull flap A downward, and outside reverse fold area B simultaneously.

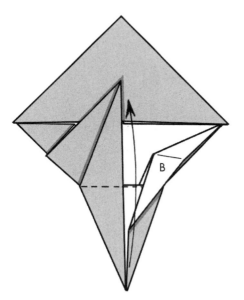

8 Valley fold flap back up.

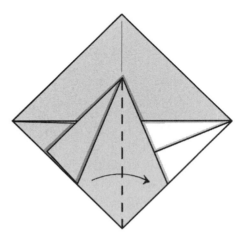

9 Valley fold the upper flap across.

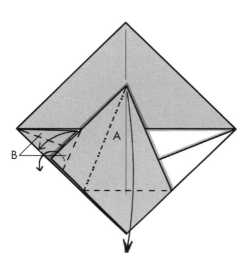

10 Similar to Step 7—pull flap A downward and outside reverse fold area B simultaneously.

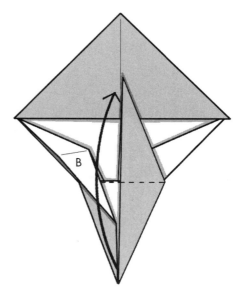

11 Valley fold flap back up.

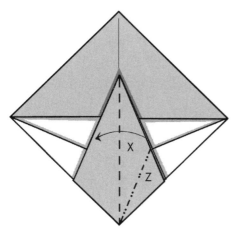

12 Fold flap X across and squash open section Z simultaneously.

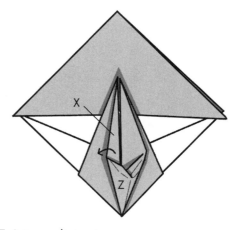

13 Intermediate step.

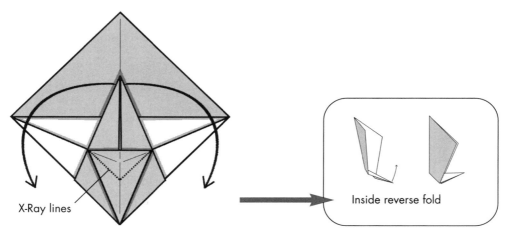

X-Ray lines

Inside reverse fold

14 Inside reverse fold arms down.

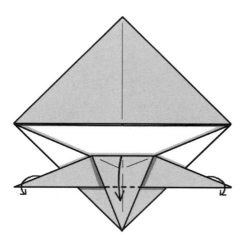

15 Valley fold front flap down.

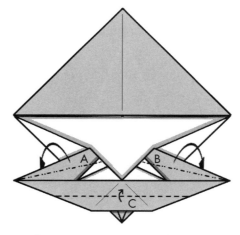

16 Inside reverse areas A and B (similar to that of a sink fold) and valley fold section C up.

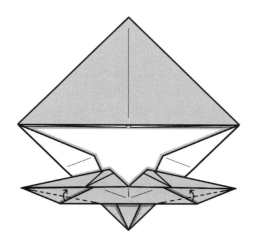

17 Valley fold the two small corner sections upward.

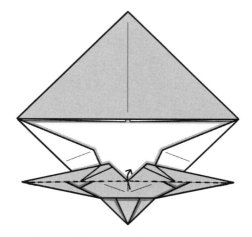

18 Valley fold the lower flap back up.

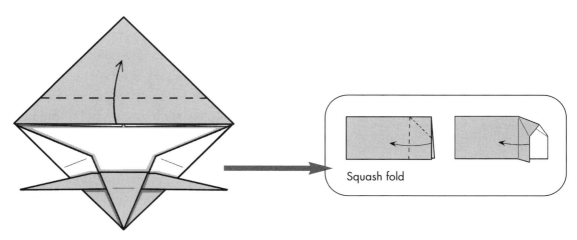

Squash fold

19 Fold front flap up, and squash open pockets underneath.

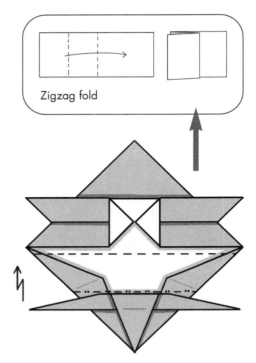

Zigzag fold

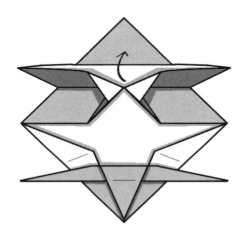

20 Intermediate step.

21 Zigzag fold the lower section upward.

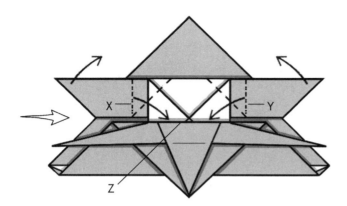

22 Fold lines X and Y onto edge Z.
TIP: The outer edges of X and Y will meet up with the outer edges of the bottom/base.

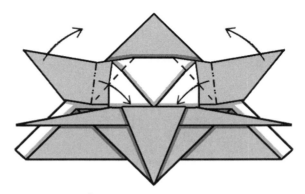

23 Intermediate step.

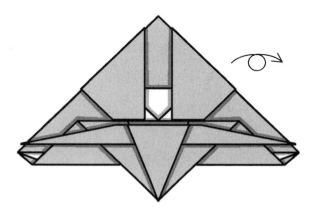

24 Turn over.

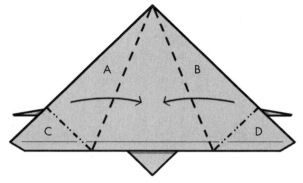

25 Valley fold areas A and B toward the center and squash open areas C and D.

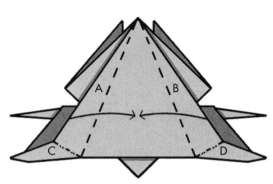

26 Intermediate step.

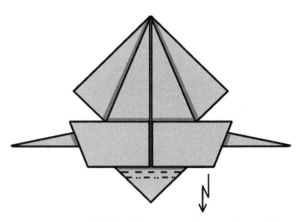

27 Zigzag fold the bottom end as indicated.

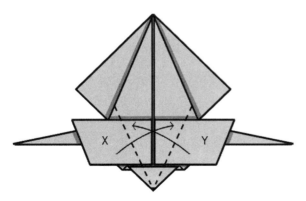

28 Valley fold flaps X and Y across.

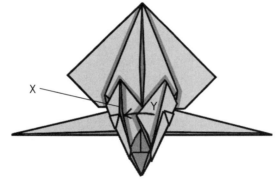

29 Insert flap Y into pocket X.

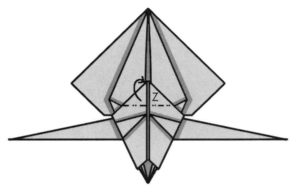

30 Hill fold corner Z back to lock the flaps together.

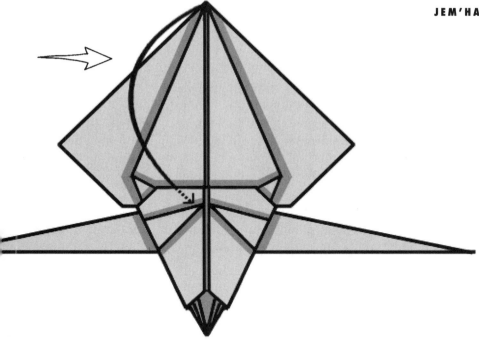

31 Roll down the front upper flap into the center pocket to form a curved body shape.

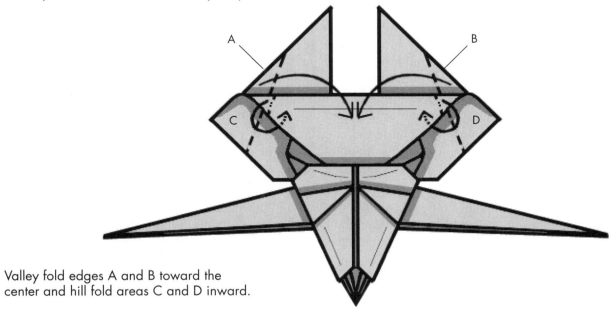

32 Valley fold edges A and B toward the center and hill fold areas C and D inward.

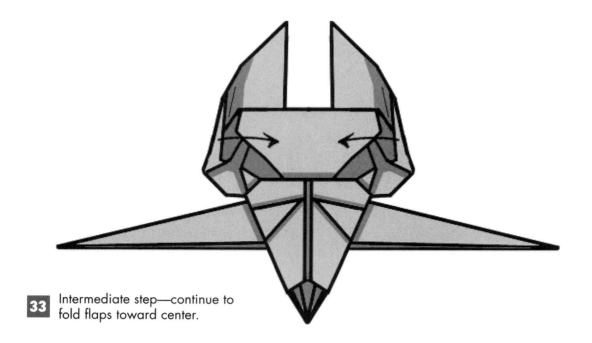

33 Intermediate step—continue to fold flaps toward center.

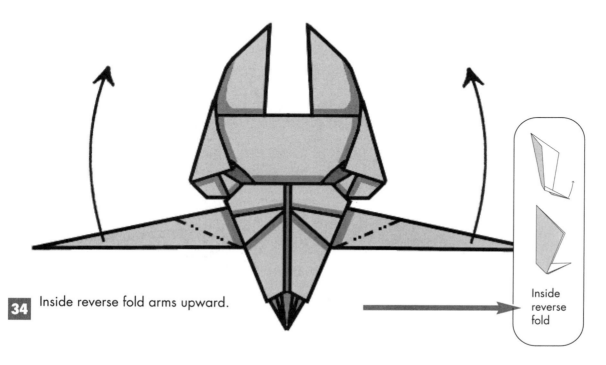

34 Inside reverse fold arms upward.

Inside reverse fold

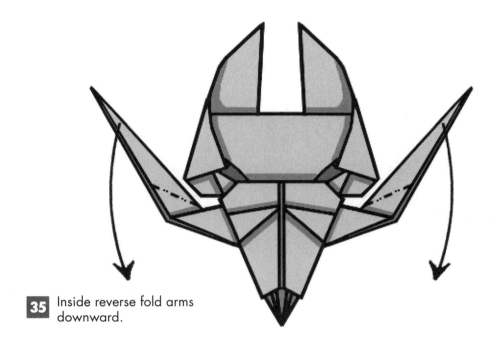

35 Inside reverse fold arms downward.

36 Outside reverse fold arms downward.

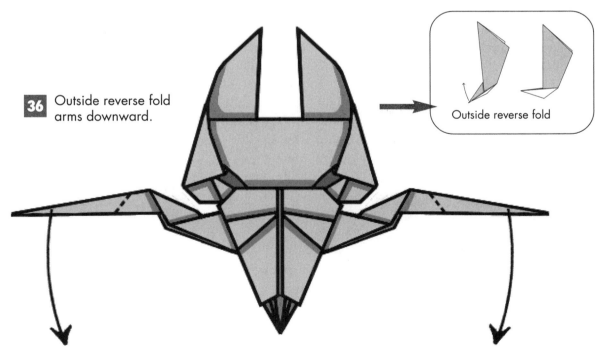

Outside reverse fold

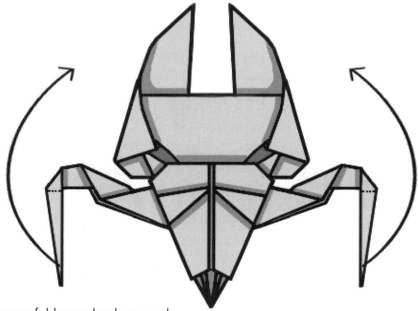

37 Outside reverse fold arms back upward.

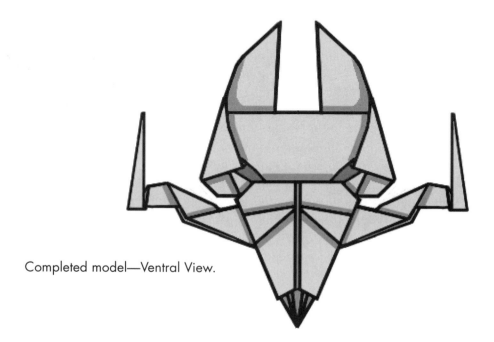

Completed model—Ventral View.

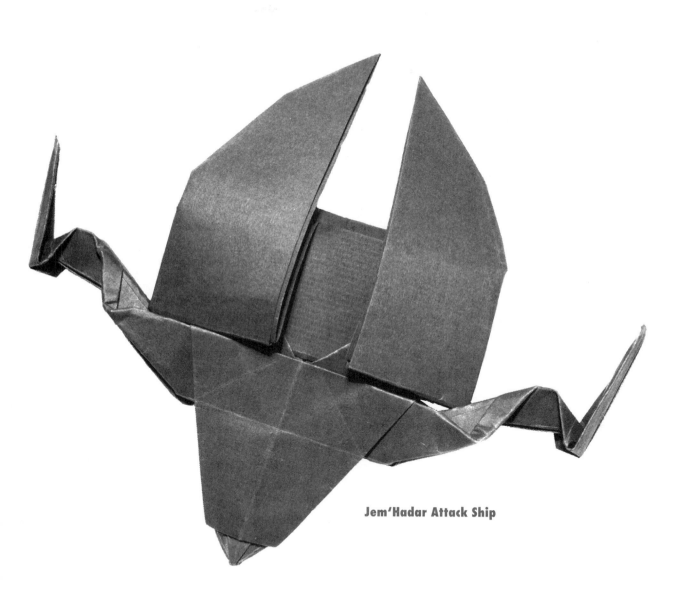

Jem'Hadar Attack Ship

Romulan Bird-of-Prey

Begin with Step 12 of Starbase 1.

Starbase 1

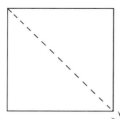

1a Begin with a square piece of paper. Make a diagonal crease and cut at dotted line to create two isosceles triangles.

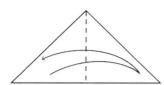

2a Take one of the triangles and precrease at the centerline. (Keep the other triangle; it will be used to fold the saucer section of the ship.)

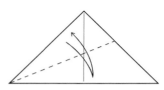

3a Valley fold the top left edge down toward the bottom edge to precrease the paper.

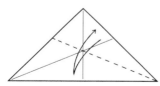

4a Repeat Step 3 on the top right edge.

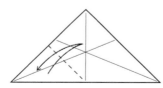

5a Valley fold the left bottom edge toward the creased centerline.

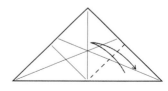

6a Repeat Step 5 on the bottom right-hand edge.

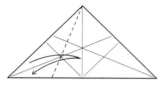

7a Valley fold the top left-hand edge toward the centerline to precrease the paper.

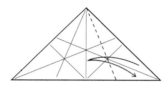

8a Repeat Step 7 on the top right-hand edge.

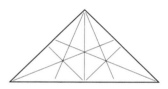

9a All the precreases are completed.

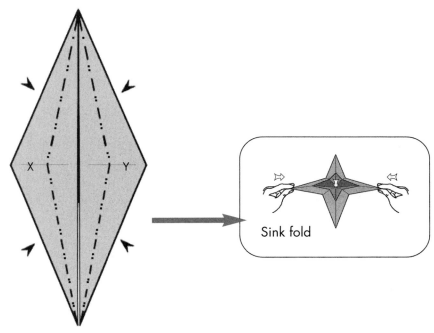

Sink fold

1 Sink in the entire sides X and Y.

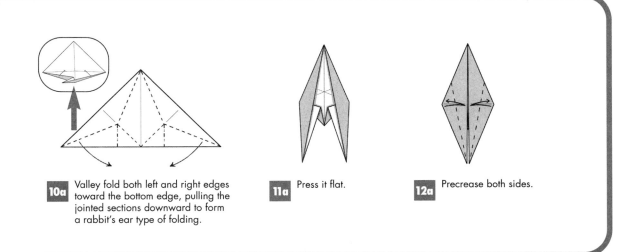

10a Valley fold both left and right edges toward the bottom edge, pulling the jointed sections downward to form a rabbit's ear type of folding.

11a Press it flat.

12a Precrease both sides.

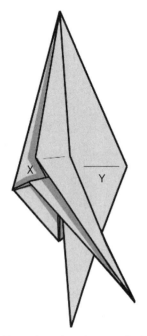

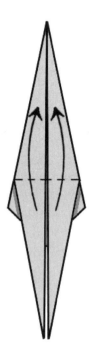

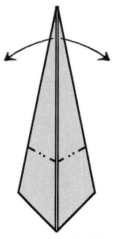

2 Completed sink on side X; repeat on side Y.

3 Valley fold both legs upward.

4 Inside reverse fold both legs outward.

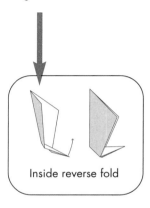

Inside reverse fold

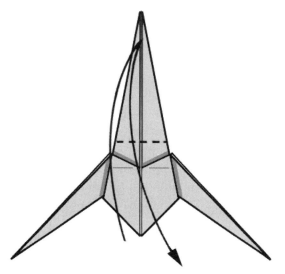

5 Precrease model as shown.

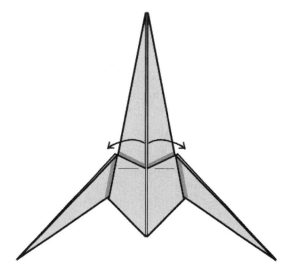

6 Open up flaps completely to reveal the inside layer.

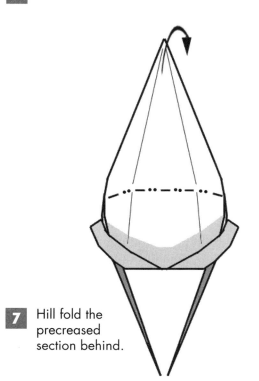

7 Hill fold the precreased section behind.

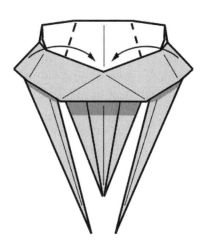

8 Gently close the flaps back toward the center.

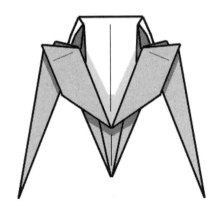

9 Intermediate step—continue to close flaps back.

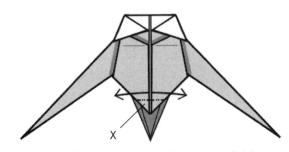

10 Open flaps up and inside reverse fold bottom tip X completely inward.

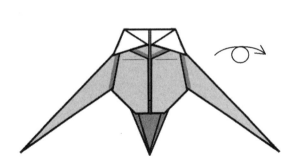

11 Turn over.

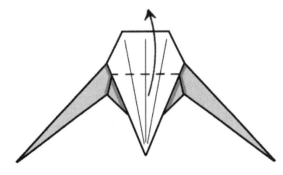

12 Fold flap upward.

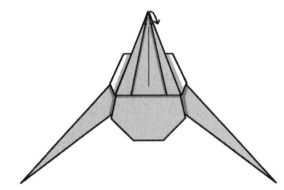

13 Hill fold the small tip section backward.

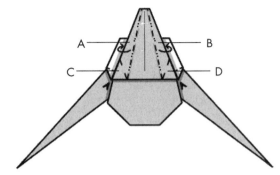

14 Hill fold areas A and B backward and squash in areas C and D simultaneously.

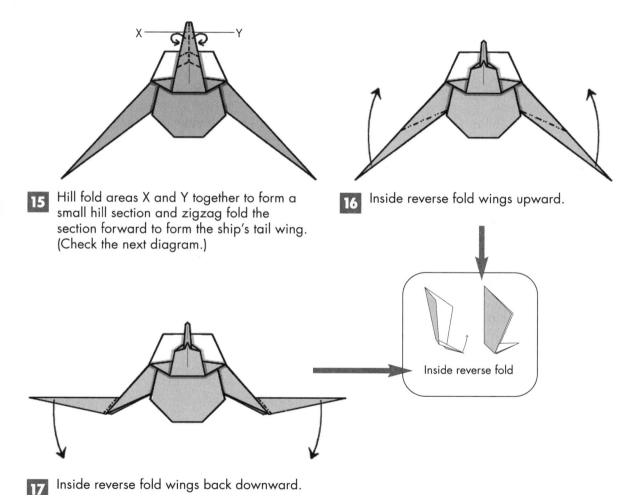

15 Hill fold areas X and Y together to form a small hill section and zigzag fold the section forward to form the ship's tail wing. (Check the next diagram.)

16 Inside reverse fold wings upward.

Inside reverse fold

17 Inside reverse fold wings back downward.

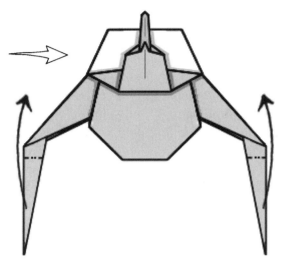

18 Inside reverse fold wings back upward again.

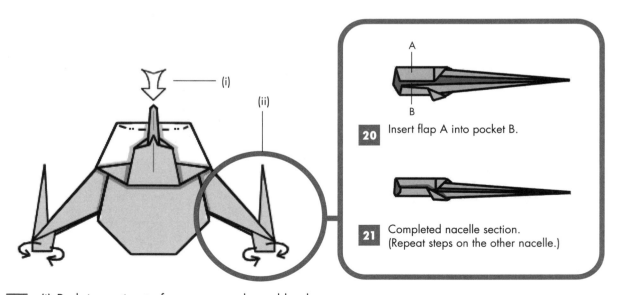

20 Insert flap A into pocket B.

21 Completed nacelle section.
(Repeat steps on the other nacelle.)

19 (i) Push in section to form a curve shaped back.
(ii) Roll the two wing nacelles into a circular shape.

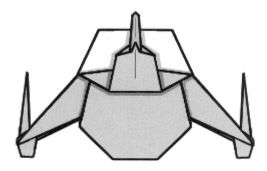

Dorsal View

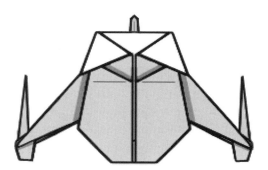

Ventral View

Romulan Bird-of-Prey

Acknowledgments

I would like to thank all my friends who have encouraged and supported me in finishing this book.

My editor, Margaret Clark, for her patience and sense of adventure.

My agent, Meredith Bernstein, for working her magic.

Paul "Woof" Grezoux, Dickie Fowler, Dean Morris, Edward Bean, Jo Fok, Pete Millward, Sidney Ko, Lisa Wu, Nick Loup, June Cheah, and Dorian "DC" Bull, for how it all got started.